M. B Cook

Japan: a Sailor's Visit to the Island empire

M. B Cook

Japan: a Sailor's Visit to the Island empire

ISBN/EAN: 9783743308183

Manufactured in Europe, USA, Canada, Australia, Japa

Cover: Foto ©ninafisch / pixelio.de

Manufactured and distributed by brebook publishing software
(www.brebook.com)

M. B Cook

Japan: a Sailor's Visit to the Island empire

A SAILOR'S VISIT TO THE ISLAND EMPIRE

BY

M. B. COOK

————

NEW YORK
JOHN B. ALDEN, PUBLISHER
1891

CONTENTS.

INTRODUCTION.

IT is with much diffidence that I send this little book afloat, well knowing that many imper-
fections are in its pages, for which I ask pardon,
and hope as a first attempt the errors may be forgiven.

On my first voyage to Japan I became very
much interested in the people and country, and
while there availed myself of every opportunity
to learn their customs, ceremonies, traditions and
legends, from the natives as well as from foreigners. This information was increased by a few
books obtained relating to the Island Empire.

With the intention of interesting my family
and a few intimate friends, I compiled from my
reading, sightseeing and tales related to me, the
following sketches to which a subsequent voyage
enabled me to make some additions, and as they
interested many friends I have been advised by
them to give my " notes " to the public. In so
doing, no claim is laid to originality aside from
what was observed in my intercourse with the
people, and I only claim to have condensed what
appeared to be the most noteworthy of whatever
was read or seen in this wonderful land.

M. B. C.

FRIENDSHIP, MAINE, 1890.

JAPAN.

CHAPTER I.

APPROACHING JAPAN---THE SACRED MOUNTAIN---
ISLAND OF OSIMA---ARRIVAL AT YOKOHAMA---
SAMPANS---ON SHORE.

ALWAYS having had a desire to visit the East,
it was a pleasant surprise, when I was called by
business in that direction, but when the Japanese
Empire was announced as my destination I felt
as one favored by the gods. The following nar-
rative of my travels is the result of my visit
there. The notes I commenced as the land was
neared, so as to convey some idea of the outlying
islands and coast from the time we passed the
volcano group, the southernmost of which lies a
few hundred miles south of Japan, where we began anxiously to count the days and hours which
must expire before we could arrive at our destined port.

Our ship drove forward through mist and fog
towards the land of the " Rising Sun," that land
which in the past had been visited only in
dreams, in which it was pictured as a fairy land,
and the people, in imagination, the elves and
fairies who peopled it. That land of wonder and
delight to every traveler, we were fast approaching, every dash of the ship against the billows,

every heave of the rolling sea was forcing us nearer to the longed for goal.

> " 'Tis a thought sublime that man can force
> A path upon the waste, can find a way
> Where all is trackless, and compel the winds
> To lend their untamed wings and bear him on
> To distant climes."

All I have ever read about this distant land was easily recalled, and the mysterious traveler, Marco Polo, can be seen exploring this unknown country and hastening back to the Western world, the first to report the existence of the rich and powerful islands of Japan. With but a slight stretch of the imagination, one can see the look of incredulity on many a listener's face as he reproduces the scenes of his wanderings and relates his adventures and the dangers he has escaped.

How easy to let the mind advance step by step until we see Pinto cast by a terrific gale upon its shores, and a few years later note a fleet of five small vessels sailing from the port of Rotterdam to discover new lands in the East and spread their commerce to all parts of this then comparatively unknown country.

We can see the English sailor, Will Adams, a true type of an ocean wanderer, among the crew, and trace him as the leader of the little band of forlorn, shipwrecked mariners when thrown upon this foreign strand, and follow him inside the prison walls, where, by his intelligence and tact, he becomes the means of his comrades' release, gaining the good will of the officers, so that by his request they are allowed to depart. We follow Adams, who, taken into the confidence of the Emperor, is raised to posts of honor and emolument. He also ingratiated himself with the Shogun (district ruler) whose residence

was near Yokuska, and was one of the first who
built Japanese vessels at that place, which has
now become the chief naval yard of Japan. Not
being allowed to return home, he married a Japanese woman by whom he left one son and one
daughter. There are some people now living at
Yokohama who claim to be his descendants.
The tomb for himself and wife was chosen by
Adams and commands a splendid view of the
navy yard, bay and surrounding country.

His burial expenses were borne by the people
by whom he was adopted, and even at this late
day on the 15th of each June the people of Tokio
meet and celebrate the day in his honor.

Then the thoughts quietly advance apace until
in July, 1853, we see our own Perry with his four
war vessels off the coast of Yedo, and his return
the following year, his fleet increased, and he
ready to negotiate a treaty of friendship, which
was successfully accomplished, and thus this far
distant Eastern land united with the great American nation of the West, and commercial and
friendly relations established which no power has
yet had the temerity to attempt to dissolve.

At last, after patient waiting, one night during
a heavy gale, the land of promise was sighted.
A few hours later as the moon broke through the
clouds, her light shone on Japan's largest mountain, whose lofty summit, snow crowned, was
dazzling in the soft moonlight, and looked like
the sacred mountain which it is to all Japanese,
the famous Fusi Yama, which

> " Like a giant stands
> To sentinel enchanted land."

This remarkable mountain cannot fail to be
distinguished from any other land upon the
coast, and has been seen by storm-tossed mari-

ners when over a hundred miles away. As the Gulf of Yedo is approached, its lofty truncated cone, 12,450 feet high, is magnificent beyond description. When the sun arose from behind the lower mountains and cast its rays over the snow clad peak, causing it to glisten, dilate and shine in all its lofty grandeur, not one of us could suppress exclamations of pleasure at so beautiful a transition. For one, I did not wonder that it was a sacred mount, to this people, and thought with pleasure, that as a noble work of the Supreme Being, it was not an unworthy object for adoration.

As we gazed, drinking in the superb scene, our hearts lifted in reverence to the Creator of this magnificent pile, the bold rocky headland of Idsu at the southern termination of the mountain peninsula of the same name came into view.

Soon the rocky island of Miko Moto was discerned, which, though small in extent, is of great importance to the sailor, as its brilliant light guides the storm driven craft into a haven of rest. This light supplies the place of beacon fires which were lighted at night on Idsu's high cape only a few short years ago. No better indication of the progress made by this people of the "Morning Land" in the last few years can be cited than the lighting of their dangerous and rocky coast. Previous to 1869, not one light was exhibited; now over fifty sent forth their rays to warn the mariner of the vicinity of rocks and land. On many an island and dangerous cape are placed those beacons of civilization of which any nation might well feel proud.

The same day we passed north of Osima, the largest and most northerly of the chain of volcanic islands lying south of Yedo Gulf. It is a remarkable, oval-shaped island, the center of which attains an elevation of 2600 feet. At its

center is an active volcano from which continually rises white, vapor-like clouds forming a halo
like a crown around its head. There is often
poured forth fire, which, mingled with the white
vapor, creates a grand transformation scene ; it
makes a deep impression on the senses, and is a
source of admiration not unmixed with awe to
the beholder. It is very conspicuous, and visible
day or night for many miles.

There are upon the island several settlements,
and on the north end a small harbor suitable for
fishing craft. The inhabitants are said to be civil
and hospitable, but have a superstitious aversion
to strangers desirous of visiting the volcano.

The sloping sides of the mountain are extensively cultivated, and the whole dotted and
checkered by numerous villages. Before night
again spread her dark mantle about us, the low
coast of Sagami had risen on the horizon and in
a short time we were skirting its shores, and glad
were we to see a pilot shoot out from between
the rocks of the coast, and his Japanese face was
hailed with pleasure as we welcomed him on
board. His eight men turned their boat to the
shore sculling lustily to a monotonous sing-song
tune by which they kept a more steady motion of
the oar as they heaved their weight against it.

With a fair wind we bowled along up Yedo
bay, passing many little villages with their neatly
thatched roofed huts, and numerous fishing boats
and junks, the fort and lights at Kanon Saki, the
navy yard at Yokuska, the grave of " Will
Adams " pointed out by the pilot, round the light-
ship, with a glance at Kanagawa at the head of
the bay, while with deepening interest we saw
the shores of Yokohama gradually displayed as
we approached, broken here and there by hills,
headlands and valleys in indescribable variety.
At last, just as the shore lights began to twinkle

in the twilight, we neared our long-looked for
goal, our anchor splashed in the water, darkness
closed around us, and the voyage occupying five
months, had ended, in which time we had traversed over twenty-one thousand miles of trackless
ocean.   It being too late to set foot on this foreign strand, we reluctantly retired to the cabin,
but found little rest in sleep, as we could only
think of Japan, with its beautiful scenery, and
we longed to explore at once the wonders of the
place.

How vividly the remembrance of the early
morn with its confused sounds comes up before
me, the babbling of the Sampan men, who, in
their boats were clustered about us, each with his
head thrown back, voice raised to its highest
pitch, shouting fourth their abilities, trustworthi-
ness and the recommendations they had received
from other ship masters by whom they had been
formerly employed, and all soliciting work for the
time the ship was to remain in port.

As soon as one is engaged, the rest acquiesce
in the choice, leave the ship, and that is the last
of their importunities.

The Sampan is a boat some sixteen feet in
length by four in breadth, flat bottomed and pro-
pelled by sculling instead of rowing. For that
purpose, outriggers cross the Sampan at regular
distances, projecting some ten inches on each
side.

The oar, in which there is a hole for the purpose, is allowed to play on a small wooden pin in
the center of the outrigger, to which the oar is
partly attached by a cord fastened in the boat
leading up through the same with a loop in the
loose end, which is put over a pin in the oar,
keeping it when in use, always at the same angle.
The natives propel their boats very fast and
some of the larger Sampans, which carry as many

as nine men, will attain a speed of seven and even
eight miles an hour. As the men heave their
weight against the oar, they repeat in concert a
gutteral sound, not unlike, " ohuk ohuk " if uttered from the lower part of the throat. To an
American, this form of propulsion is the first
thing noticed, even where all is wonderful.

Many things, especially labor, are very cheap,
still we heard of no strikes, and all seemed contented and happy. May it be long years in the
future before they become enough civilized to
adopt the policy of some of our laborers as they
now practice it in enlightened America. For the
sum of seventy-five sens (cents) per day, a good
Sampan was employed, managed by two men ;
the boat was well kept, always neat and clean,
the men ready night or day, and always attentive
and accommodating. When their term of service
had expired, instead of begging for the drinks or
cigars, they each brought a small present as a
keepsake and to show their gratitude for their
employment.

At last we had time to look about us and were
lost in admiration of the scenery, which is beautiful in all directions.

In the harbor were ships of many nations,
and we beheld the flag of Japan proudly floating
from a number of her war ships, among the rest,
an iron clad frigate, which any nation might be
glad to call her own. Away to the west, the
lordly Fusi rears its head, and we are surprised to
find we have passed more than half way around
it, as yesterday it was seen away to the East,
while to-day the rising sun casts his splendor on
its snowy crown in the West.

Our eyes look for objects nearer our situation
and we see Yokohama, " the City of the Plain "
surrounded by low hills directly in our front.
Its stately edifices rise majestically above the

generally flat houses of the Japanese, presenting a contrast noticeable to every traveler.

We can see the canals which traverse the city and learn afterward that they entirely surround and isolate it from communication with the interior except by crossing bridges and causeways.

As soon as the usual routine prescribed for a foreign vessel was complied with, we started for the shore, and in a few moments were at the landing, our feet pressing the " Land of the Rising Sun."

Some one has said "To pass from one great kingdom to another, forms an epoch in most men's lives."

A new government, language, and climate are all, for a time, objects of wonder as well as interest ; but the change between two of earth's most distant quarters is indeed an exciting transition.

A long stone pier extending into the sea forms a breakwater and affords an excellent landing which we soon tread with our weary sea-tossed feet, rejoicing that we stand upon the soil of the distant East, and have commenced that round of travels which will ever be in memory the most delightful of our existence. I never shall forget the thrill of pleasure which pervaded my whole being when I first landed in Japan—a region how glorious, how beautiful, how grand !

This is a land of wonder and romance which has been until lately as a sealed book, but now like other nations is rapidly developing, while it still retains its own perception of beauty and its own ideals toward which all its works tend. It must not be forgotten that when the country was finally opened to foreigners, they discovered a people under a settled government, and a civilization of their own, although like themselves peculiar.

Revolutions were in progress causing a near resemblance in government to the condition of some of our South American republics.

The people, who are usually small and slender, are remarkable for their agility and skill, and excel in execution as well as invention, the truth of which much of their curious work in fancy arti- cles will attest.

CHAPTER II.

FROM the first moment in which we set foot upon land until our departure, not a day passed which did not bring to our sight something new, novel and interesting. Among the first things noticed as we entered the town was a line of jin-rikisha men with their hand-carriages waiting for a job. The shafts of these two-wheeled vehicles are resting on the ground, while their owners are standing by or sitting on the sloping seat. Their dress consists generally of a blue shirt with wide hanging sleeves tucked in at the waist, and tight fitting breeches of the same color reaching just below the knee. The feet are bare, except that straw sandals are fastened on by means of a cord passing around the ankle and between the toes to keep them in place.

Most of them in winter have a red blanket about their shoulders, which is transferred to the knees of the person by whom they are employed, while they start up at a brisk trot, often passing horses on their journeys, and will continue at a rapid gait for hours. The jinrikisha is the common carriage of Japan and is easy and comfortable. They have a covered top like an American chaise, of which, in fact, they are a miniature, so that one can always be sheltered from rain or sun. When used about the city they are always hauled by one person, but when on long journeys two men are generally employed. It is said that more than thirty thousand of these little carriages are in use in the city of Tokio alone, and that over two hundred thousand find employment in Japan.

The jinrikisha men, as a class, are the most rascally fellows in Japan, but as they know all that will interest a foreigner, and have picked up enough English to make themselves understood, they are invaluable, and an excursion into the surrounding country without them loses half its interest and charm.

I never shall forget the first ride in one of those little carriages the morning I made my advent among the people of Japan. With a rapid pace I was whirled to my consignees and the custom house, and afterwards to my compradore, Mr. Collyer, an American, by whom I was at once made to feel at home, and to whom I am much indebted for kindness and advice, as well as for many hours spent in his company, replete with information about the customs and manners of his adopted land.

Yokohama is one of the most frequented ports in Japan. When Commodore Perry opened this port, it was composed only of a few stray huts which, as late as 1859, had become only an insignificant fishing village in the midst of a marsh. Across the bay was Kanagawa, the town which was named by the treaty to be opened to foreign trade in July, 1859. Yokohama, being a place of much greater convenience as a shipping port, the place grew and increased daily, until finally, by evasion of the letter of the treaty, it became the actual port of entry.

In 1862 it contained only 126 foreigners, which in 1888 had increased to over 4000, half of which are Chinese. The native element muster about

125,000, their city covering a large territory.
The town extends along a level shore, but is
backed by a circle of low wooded hills. Those
lying southeast of the town are denominated the
" Bluff," and are occupied by Americans and
Europeans as a settlement.

In most cases their residences are very pleas-
antly located, and their tastefully laid out gardens
present a cheerful appearance. A walk to the
Bluff on a clear morning will well repay an observer, as he will obtain an unsurpassed view of
the settlement, the bay and surrounding country,
as well as of the beautiful gardens and groves of
ornamental trees in and about the city. The
roadway, which divides the foreign from the Japanese settlement, is broad and spacious, with
wide sidewalks, (which, however, are scarcely
ever occupied, most people taking the street
center), and then a space of some thirty feet or
more in depth devoted to ornamental trees and
flowering shrubs, peculiar to Japan, along which
is an evergreen hedge marking the inner line of
the sidewalk. The street is macadamized, well
rounded in the center, and always kept neat and
clean.

At every step the observer takes in the native
town of Yokohama, he will find something of
interest. There are some temples of note, one of
which is situated on Noge Yama (a high hill west
of the city, and overlooking it), of the Shinto religion, which possesses some celebrity.

The shops on the main street (Honcho Dori),
contain immense quantities of lacquered ware,
bronzes, ivory, carved in beautiful and fantastic
figures, porcelain and many curios, not forgetting
fans of all shapes, sizes and material.

The silk stores exhibit beautiful specimens of
native ingenuity in embroidery and other needle
work. In the remote part of the city are exten-

sive manufactories of porcelain and lacquer ware. One of the principal and most interesting streets, with an unpronounceable name, is devoted to theatres, tea houses, baths, shooting galleries, restaurants and other places of amusement. One night, in company with a friend, we visited a restaurant, where probably we were the first Americans who had ever honored their place of business. My friend, who could command a few words of Japanese, called for beefsteak, which, after long waiting, we found still in the stall below, the proprietor waiting for a cash deposit before presenting the food.

Immediately on receiving the advance, the steak was brought, when behold, it was cut into small pieces just fitted for the mouth and perfectly raw. With the first waitress (and, by the way, the attendants are all girls, and pretty ones, too), came another bringing an "hibachi" or brasier full of lighted coals, with spider and tongs, closely followed by another with salt, pepper, and other condiments. They deposited their loads, including a supply of chopsticks, and then suddenly left us to do our own cooking, which we so well performed that a second steak was required. Tea having been drank, and the very moderate charge settled, we were bowed out with many a graceful motion and "arigatoes" (Thank you). Many times afterward while passing this saloon, we were accosted by one of the waiter girls, who, running into the street and looking up into our faces with a pleading look, would repeat the only word of English she knew, *beefsteak*.

The shooting galleries were often visited, and every time a good natured crowd would gather about, and when a good shot was made, the cry "yoroshii, yoroshii" (good, good), would resound throughout the crowd, and then all of them

would want to shake hands with the (okii) (big)
Americans.

The tea booths, which were at almost every
corner, were always interesting to visit. Most of
them are connected with an archery where
twenty-five arrows could be disposed of for a few
cents, after which would always follow a cup of
colorless Japan tea and sweatmeats, the amount
of pay being left to the generosity of the guest.
The small sum of ten cents would amply satisfy,
but if in a more generous mood, twice that sum
is given, you are well repaid by the profuse
thanks and fervid expressions this class will lav-
ish upon you. If in your simplicity you give
them more than you intend, no change will be
returned, as all tea houses are supported by the
gifts of visitors, so nothing is ever returned, no
change made. If you insist you will be assailed
with " yukeyo ojiisan," (go away, old man), and
their politeness is turned to railing as quickly as
the fisherwoman of England would return banter
with brawling.

The girls are generally of less than twenty
years of age, bright and comely, but have contrived to spoil, while no doubt they think they
have enhanced their beauty by painting their lips
a bright vermilion, making themselves, in a manner, uniform, and it is as much the custom as it
is for married ladies to paint their teeth black.
The more entertaining the girls, the more likely
you are to come away minus something, especially
handkerchiefs, as they are adepts in all the archery booths at purloining that article.

Next in number to the tea booths are the
baths, which can be distinguished by glass doors
checkered with small panes of colored glass.
There one can enjoy the luxury at the public
fount in company with whole families, or if his
modesty is above mingling in the water with

naked heathens, a private bath is at his disposal,
where he can enjoy himself in hot or cold, salt or
fresh water, at a nominal price. The public
baths can be entered for a penny, and it is indeed
this extremely low price which allows so many
natives to visit them. If the old proverb that
" cleanliness is next to godliness" is true, the
Japanese surely come very nearly to godliness,
for none can deny that they are scrupulously
neat and clean, and they are never seen on the
street or in the house without looking as if they
had just left the bath ; the ladies are never seen
unless their hair is elaborately dressed, and they
always look as though they had come from the
laundry and the barber.

Theatres, with their gaudy flags and loud-
mouthed ushers at the door cannot fail to attract
attention, but they are not generally interesting,
neither are they beautiful in finish or decoration,
but are unlike anything else in Japan, being
cheap and tawdry in all their designs. The
plays, which are chiefly tragedy, are very long,
and consist of long harangues by the stars, sometimes of an half hour each without any other
actor on the stage. As a general thing, ladies
are not allowed to act, their parts being represented by the lords of creation. The end of the
piece is usually frightful, and not at all what an
American is likely to admire. The whole consists of many parts or scenes, which often takes
from early morn till dewy eve to perform, with
only a short intermission for lunch. It was my
good fortune to receive an invitation from a
Japanese lady and gentleman to visit a new
theatre just opened in Yokohama, where the
celebrated historical play of the " Forty-seven
Ronins " was to be acted.

So at ten o'clock A. M. we were at the door,
and were soon crowding our way to the second

floor, where a box had been procured for our party. The box proved to be only a reserved space in the centre, around which a temporary railing had been placed. The seats were the usual square cushions laid upon the floor upon which we were soon squatting.

A comical position for a man of six feet! The play was in progress, and being familiar with the old legend, I could follow it most of the time, with a few words of explanation from my Japanese friends. In some parts the acting was fine, and the costumes of the nobles were elegant. There was not a break in the play or any lengthened stop, until four P. M. when all the paraphernalia of the stage was quickly removed and the managers declared an half hour for lunch.

This we all indulged in at a restaurant across the way, after which we returned on board while our friends went back to the play. The next day they informed us that it finished at eleven P. M., that the play, as we at home might say, was a great "hit," and the star a noted actor. The length of time occupied by the troupe was considered the highest recommendation the play could obtain.

All this could be witnessed from a reserved seat for twenty sens (cents), or from the family circle for half that amount. I was told that when the final scene was too horrible to present to the audience, the villain to whom punishment is decreed, retires from view into a side room, over the door of which there is a representation of the blossoms of a plum or cherry tree. First one and then another of the blossoms is seen to fall, and finally the whole in a sudden shower, which tells to the waiting Japs that justice is satisfied,—the play is over.

CHAPTER III.

THE guide book says, "no tourist should leave
Japan without visiting Kamakura, Dai Butsu and
Enoshima, around which every spot of ground is
classic to the Japanese, and many of their histo-
ries and tales of romance have their scenes laid
in and about this vicinity."

So, taking advantage of an introduction to the
daughter of an old Daimio, a young princess in
the peculiar political relationship which the people held with the former Mikado (or rather in
the reign of his Shogunate), we induced her and
one of her friends to accompany us as companions and guides.

A fine morning found us at the Yokohama
station, where we embarked on the train for
Fujisawa, a little village on the Tokaido road,
fifteen miles distant, and the nearest stopping
place to this classic spot. Having the wonders
of the different localities pointed out as we
slowly rode along, the time passed quickly, so
that we were soon at the end of our railroad
journey.

We then changed our propelling power from
the mighty engine driven by steam, for the
diminutive little two-wheeled carriage, called the
jinrikisha, usually drawn by one man, which in
our case, as the journey was to be long, was

increased to two. Soon we were in motion, going at a rapid rate, bound for the gigantic statue of the great Japanese idol, Dai Butsu, or great Buddha.

We entered the lovely valley of Kamakura, by the north road, which is cut through a rocky mountain, the tall cliffs of solid rock rising some three hundred feet on either side, and extending nearly a mile from entrance to exit. The labor performed here is almost incalculable, but was carried forward persistently, as there was no way of getting into this valley from the north and only one road each from the east and west, while the south was open to the sea.

As we emerged from the rocky cut we were at once led to admire the wonderful view of the beautiful valley and its sea-washed shores, while in a moment, on rounding a sharp turn we were brought face to face with the colossal statue we had come to visit. This image is said by some to be the largest and most famous piece of casting in Japan. It is fifty-two feet high, and nearly as broad at the shoulders as it is long, and measures ninety-eight feet about the waist. It is not known when the image was set up and there is much tradition regarding it. . As early as A. D. 1200, it is reported to have been thrown down by a tidal wave, and a temple by which it was then covered, totally destroyed. The material is an alloy of copper, tin and gold, five hundred pounds of the most precious metal having been used. Near the idol are huge pieces of copper representing the petals of the lotus flower and which it was supposed formed the base on which the casting rested before the tidal wave. The lotus is sacred to the Buddhist Japanese, and according to their ideas, the purified soul in the Buddhist paradise meditates and rests on the lotus flower.

Inside were many gilt idols and numerous twisted vows and prayers on paper, ready to sell to the devout. The old priest who attends the image is very attentive and shows you up the winding stairs to the Buddha's head, where he will sell you a prayer for a few sens, or conduct you to the lower story and there dispense photographs and beer.

One soon learns that this monstrous god is not too sacred to cause a penny to fall into the holy priest's pocket. After a thorough view of the inside and an observation obtained from under the frown of the god's mighty brow, while sitting on his thumbs, we descended to the foot, where we invested in photographs of the place and the beautiful surroundings, then we sipped from a Japanese tea-bowl, tea concocted by one of the tea-house girls, who are allowed to carry on their traffic under the shade of this most revered idol.

We gave a few cents to the priest in charge to procure his blessing when we started our teams for the grand temple of Hachiman, the god of war. Our road lay in the direction of the ancient capital. The whole neighborhood through which we passed, may be considered the Richmond of Japan, for scores of battles have been fought and streams of blood have flowed in the different struggles for its possession.

This noted temple, Hachiman, is situated on the north road, the approach to which is through a wide avenue of stately trees and groves of the graceful bamboo and through numerous great gateways called torii. This entrance way is universal at all the temples and public buildings unless of very modern construction, and is also the only way into many private residences. It appears to be erected as an approach to superior authorities as well as an emblem of respect to both the visited and the visitor.

Hachiman stands on an elevated plateau, reached by some sixty granite steps, in the immediate front of which is a plot of earth beaten solid to be used on festival occasions by musicians and dancers who perform the sacred dances, emblematical of the Shinto religious rites to which sect this temple is dedicated. At the right of the edifice is a massive tree said to be over one thousand years old. It is an Icho tree under the branches of which the grandson of the first Shogun (chief), Yorotomo, was killed, by whose death, that line of princes became extinct.

Several large stones about the temple are supposed to possess some sacred influence ; one has a very singular natural figure on its surface. Two others placed under the big Icho tree are worshiped by barren women and are worn as smooth as glass, having been occupied as seats so often.

About this place are many small temples and near the main edifice was one of beautiful design in process of erection.

The chief deity of Hachiman is Ojin, the son of the Empress Jingo Kogo, who conquered Corea in the third century. He was deified at his death and is now worshiped under the above name. Almost every village in Japan has a temple in his honor. Quite a museum is connected with the temple, and various ancient relics have been preserved by the priests and are deposited in the safe and sacred places of the building. Those of greatest note and interest to the traveler who has read the history of this wonderful people, are the articles of war and apparel once belonging to Yorotomo, who made this place, Kamakura, the political capital of Japan in 1196 A. D.

In the court yard which encloses the buildings are cloister like compartments containing the

royal palanquins, filigree work and many grotesque masks used at their religious dances.
Among the many interesting articles are three
swords, one belonging to Yorotomo. The blades
are laquered to prevent rust, while two of the scab-
bards are of pure silver inlaid with gold. The
other, of wood, is gold lacquered and inlaid with
pearls, while the sword has a beaten silver hilt-
piece.

There are others beautifully and richly ornamented in gold, silver and precious gems, but
none are held in so much reverence as those once
used by the founder of the capital, at this place.
All the swords were made by noted makers in
Japan, those made in the province of Sagami
being held in highest repute. Here also may be
seen Yorotomo's hunting suit and battle conch,
and an elaborately inlaid chased writing-box
presented to him by a former Emperor or Mikado.

A little to the west of the main temple, in a
separate enclosure tastefully laid out and decorated, stands a shrine in Yorotomo's honor, while
a few steps east of the temple, at the head of a
flight of steps, is his tomb, which receives nearly
as much attention as the temple itself.

Here we also viewed with interest and pleasure
the noted Nichiren's writing and ink stone, besides many other warlike and ecclesiastical relics.
This eminent priest, Nichiren, was the founder
of a certain sect of Buddhists, and is regarded as
a prophet by many Japanese. He was born in a
little town on the opposite coast called Kominto,
and was very celebrated during the thirty years
preceding 1250 A. D., at which time he resided
at Kamakura.

Many miracles are attributed to his intercession
with the gods of his sect, and are related with
apparent belief by his followers. During his

residence here a hard contested engagement took place on the borders, near the little town of Inamara Saki, for the possession of Kamakura, when he was so unfortunate as to be captured by the advancing column. He was taken across a small stream called Yukiai Gawa, meaning "a place of meeting," the name being given on account of the following incident When Nichiren was about to be beheaded near Katase, the executioner raised his sword to strike, but as it was about to descend it broke in three parts, leaving the saintly priest unharmed. Amazed at the miracle, a message was sent to Kamakura to urge a reprieve. The Lord of Kamakura had repented of the sentence passed on the holy man and had sent an order for his pardon. The two messengers met at the above named brook, hence its name.

The miracle is a favorite subject among Japanese painters, and a picture of a kneeling saint with the pieces of the broken sword forming a halo about his head is seen in many a window. The now unpretentious village of Kamakura which could be seen from Hachiman, and, at one time must have been a large city, at present contains only the ruins of the royal residences of many famous rulers.

As it had been the capital of the empire for over four hundred years, we made hasty visit along the splendid roads, and through beautiful scenery, and although the principal buildings had been destroyed, they were replaced by straw roofed huts. Clean and neat was their appearance, but they do not show any of the former magnificence, as the contrast is between straw and marble, thatch and granite.

The name Kamakura means "sickle storehouse," and was given to the place as early as 669 A. D. by the Mikado's prime minister, Tariko, who, while on a pilgrimage, spent the night near the present site and was told in a dream to bury or lay in store a precious sickle, which he carried with him. He did so and was blessed therefore so that his descendants ruled the district many generations. Now all of its former greatness has departed, and the scene is most vividly recalled by the remembrance of many indescribable odors not at all agreeable to an American nose. From the streets of Kamakura we drove to the Kaihinin, a large hotel or marine sanitarium facing the sea, and surrounded by beautiful walks and drives. In the summer season it is full of guests, and being in one of the most healthy places in Japan, and the visitors are given so much attention, that it is becoming a center of attraction to all American tourists. An excellent meal prepared in European manner was soon devoured, when we retired to the waiting room to give our teams a longer rest.

We were followed by a little girl of six or seven summers who entertained us with music from an instrument called the *koto*, which she accompanied with her wee small voice. The *koto* was about five feet long, not over four inches high at the ends, rounding up toward the middle until the center was about twice that height. Strings similar to those used for a guitar were stretched from end to end, and there were thirteen of them. It was tuned by separate movable bridges placed wherever the tension was required. The sound was not musical, but weird and ghastly, like a far off, melancholy murmur. The instrument is held in much repute by the Japanese, and it takes the place with them in music, that the piano does with us.

Our human teams having fed and rested, we soon had them in harness and on the way towards our destination, Enoshima, pausing by the roadside to visit the temple Riukoji, situated in the village of Koshigoye, where the relics of Nichiren are preserved. At this place is also the tomb of a man who was said to have had sixteen children devoured by a mythical dragon which formerly occupied a cave in this vicinity.

A long line of priests was busy reciting their ritual, beating drums, ringing bells, sounding gongs and repeating over and over again the meaningless words "Namu, Amida, Butsu," which is a distinctive prayer used by the Buddhist sect who are followers of the teachings of Nichi-ren.

Our princess, who had resisted her inclinations at other temples to join in the worship, probably for fear of exciting our mirth, could no longer resist temptation, but bent her knee and raised her hands so quickly in adoration to the large image, that the act was scarcely noticed by our party.

There was some beautifully carved work about the altar, resplendent in gold and lacquer. For the payment of a small sum the attendant priest opened the inside shrine, and I had a chance to gaze upon two little gold idols, each representing some noted deity, and then the gates of Paradise were opened for us to enter. The gongs sounded, drums again beat, and as each sound was wafted aloft, it became a prayer to protect me through life, as well as an advance courier which gave me a passport to their heaven. Afterwards I learned that these golden gods were stolen from Corea on one of their many marauding expeditions to that country.

Near this place is a small cluster of houses on a hill of moderate elevation, famous for the varied character of scenery displayed around and about its one small temple. Shading this insignificant place of worship is an immense pine tree called " fling-away-the-pencil-pine " because a noted Japanese artist who had come to sketch the grand scenery, flung away his brush in despair, seeing how impossible it was to transfer to his canvas the beauty he saw about him.

Advancing a short distance, we stopped at an old temple near Katase called Otomo, an edifice of but little architectual pretension, from which we were turning away in disgust, when our guide motioned us to the rear of the building, where, guarded by a shaven-headed priest we found a hole for a door, into which we were invited to enter. It was a vast space where no ray of light, except through the door, could penetrate to illuminate the gloomy scene.

Soon two priestly tapers were lighted and placed in lanterns which were already attached to ropes leading to the top of the structure. As they were hoisted into the darkness, the pulleys gave a mournful howl, as if departed demons were striving to resist the light. As soon as they reached the top, and our eyes could pierce the gloom, we found ourselves before one of the largest as well as one of the most horrible looking gods we had yet seen. It was some sixty feet high, built in about the right proportions for the body of a human being, minus the legs. The face was twisted into the most grotesque shapes, while the expression was the most hideous imaginable. This great work was of wood, covered entirely with gold leaf, so that when the swinging lights struck aright, it shone like a structure of fire. What it was made to represent, or for what purpose it was kept in this dark place, we could not learn. No doubt it represented some of their ancient rulers or imaginary ones, as every place in Japan seems to be well supplied with idols, in many cases fashioned to commemorate the name of some noted man of the past, or else to keep in remembrance some legend of her early days.

Again we moved on our way along the sea-shore, which was rolling its surf and foam nearly to our feet, and threatening to undermine the high cliffs about whose base we wound. At this point a splendid panorama breaks upon the sight. To the south, in the blue distance, was the island of Osima, with a crown of volcanic smoke about its lofty head, while to the west lay the mountains of Idzu. Landward were the peaks of Oyama, with many a lesser mount, but above all, in full magnificence of proportion was Fusi, the lordly mountain.

A little to the right, so fair and lovely, clothed in perpetual green, lay the island of Enoshima, our point of destination for the day. This is only an island at high water or whenever the wind blows hard from the sea. The rising of this causeway which connects this romantic spot with the main land at Katase, has been woven into the history of·Japan and is thus related: Nitta Yoshiada, a valorous and devoted vassal of the Emperor Godaigo, was marching against the Lord of Kamakura and his clan. An army filled the passes into the valley, blocking the march by land, while the galleys of the Hojo (Lord) pre-vented his passing this point of land, which ex-tended into the sea and was encompassed by many war craft. The case was critical if not hopeless, and his whole army doubted their ability to pass the point while the fleet was so near. Nitta hav-ing great faith in Kami (the gods) sacrificed and prayed to them the whole night, then, in the presence of his followers, solemnly cast the sword given him by the Mikado into the sea as a prayer offering, asking that the waves might recede.

When the sun arose the tide had ebbed, caus-

ing the galleys to move out into the bay so far
that their arrows could not reach the invading
host. They, believing that the gods had favored
their commander marched resistlessly forward
over the dry beach of sand, met the Hojo, and
gained a complete victory. Kamakura was taken
and the power of the ruler forever broken. It is
said that over seven thousand of the clan were
slain or killed themselves by committing "hara
kiri" (disemboweling).

Since that time this narrow strip of land has
connected the island with the main, except when
very heavy storms break through and for a short
time sever the connection.

A picture of Nitta casting his sword into the
sea now adorns the back of the two dollar paper
notes of the Japanese government.

CHAPTER IV.

ENOSHIMA — PENCIL SPONGE — BENTEN THE
BEAUTIFUL — LEGENDS —THE CAVES — BACK
TO YOKOHAMA.

As the shades of night began to gather about
us, we drove over the sandy stretch of coast, and
were soon passing up the steep incline in the
main street of the beautiful Island of Enoshima.
The name signifies Bay Island, so called on
account of its proximity to Kamakura Bay. It
rises almost perpendicular on all sides from its
ocean bed. Its rocky flanks and crest are always
clothed in dense masses of evergreen foliage.

The entrance to the summit is guarded by a
great gateway, thence you toil up a narrow,
steep street, both sides of which are lined with
shops, where shells and variegated spoils of the
sea are exposed for sale. Among other curiosi-
ties are many specimens of a peculiar sponge, or
" wonderful glass thread," found only in the deep
water of this coast. It grows with its glassy
cable downwards and the soft sponge floating
above. The Japanese call it, when rendered into
English, " pencil cord " and " sponge brush."

In the waters about the island are many huge
crabs, and one in the little museum attached to
the temple on the hill, measured twelve feet between the tips of its outstretched claws.

When almost half way to the top we turned off
to a hotel, where we were quickly met by the
host, his wife, waiters and attendants, who re-

peated after their master the stereotyped phrase
" Yoku irasshai mashta," meaning " You are welcome," to which our guide replied, "Arigato,"
("Thank you,") when we, in imitation of our
conductors, commenced to take off our shoes before entering our allotted rooms.

Cushions were quickly brought for us to sit
upon, and a charcoal fire in a large brasier to
warm our hands, about which we all gathered.
As soon as we were comfortably warm, tea and
cakes were brought in and in a short time we
were feeling quite at home in our novel situation.

While we were waiting for our supper to be
brought in, the host sent an old Japanese story
teller to entertain us, and the story he related
about the origin of this island, which was interpreted by our companions, I think of interest
enough to repeat. " Long, long years ago, a
great storm arose at night, in which heavy black
clouds covered the sea and the waves mounted
to heaven. In the morning, celestial music was
heard, and there appeared in a rift in the cloud,
a lovely lady of divine form, accompanied by
two boys of surpassing beauty. Then the storm
ceased, the black clouds lifted, and the beautiful
island of Enoshima appeared, upon the top of
which sat the heavenly lady.

She was Benten, and is believed to be the
mistress and tamer of dragons. Huge dragons
were in the great marshes about the place, which
used to destroy many children, but since that
time when the goddess sprang up, the ravages
have ceased.

As the story ended, our supper was brought
to us in numerous lacquered trays, well filled with
food, and well served by the waiters. Course
after course was placed before us, but nothing
could be found to tempt the appetites of our

party except the nicely fried fish which comprised one of the courses. Almost everything served consisted of fish in some form, as the Japs are very fond of that dish, and it is said they cook the finny tribe in the most delicious ways.

Their way of cooking and compounding may suit their taste, but when it came to boiled fresh fish, without salt, mixed with boiled beans, and well hashed together, then covered with a sour sauce somewhat thicker than molasses, the stomach of the foreign element in our party, rebelled at once.

Our guides seeing our want of European food, ordered some eggs, which were quickly brought, accompanied by a frying pan and charcoal fire upon which to cook the same, which was soon done by one of the ladies of our company. Nothing could have caused us to receive more attention than the fact that we were Americans, while our Japanese companion, who wore the badge of her rank, conspicuously, was a Daimio's daughter, whose claim to royal dignity still entitles those of that rank, to great respect from the rural Japanese, and in our case it was cheerfully accorded.

It is said that a well taught waitress will never place food or anything else before a visitor, without assuming a sitting posture, and also before asking or replying to a question she places herself in that position. This certainly was the case with our servant Belle, as one of our party soon commenced to call her.

After our feast, warm salt water baths were prepared which we were invited to enter, but the vivid remembrance of the scalding experienced in the same place a year before deterred at least one of our number.

After the remains of our supper had been removed, as well as all pertaining to the same, bedding was brought in and spread upon the floor in one corner of the room. This consisted of many thickly wadded quilts (eight) very heavy, and covered with a thick, coarse silk material. The usual block of wood for a pillow, was changed for a roll of some hard substance covered with a white cloth upon which they poured out vials, not of wrath, but perfume.

On this bed, or rather by the side of it, was laid a large silk wadded coat, which you slip into, putting your arms into the long sleeves, then draw it about you, and find yourself protected from colder weather than is often experienced in the country.

Everything being prepared, the outside shutters by which our rooms were surrounded, were closed ; large paper lanterns in each of which was a wick swimming in oil, were lighted and left with us to burn during the night. Then our waitress, the gentle Belle, gracefully seated herself on the floor in Japanese fashion, and repeated the formula " ayasumi nasai," (goodnight) bowed her head to the floor, and in a moment we were alone.

What wonder if thoughts of the long voyage came flying through my brain, the distance we were from our own loved land, the many incidences of the passage, the odd and beautiful things we had seen, the strange manners and customs of this attractive and inventive people ? I tried to realize that we were in their midst, among the people of the most rural portion of Japan ; that we had supped on the food prepared in their style, and tried to eat with chopsticks, but signally failed. Even now we were reclining on their native beds, the sacred shrine of their household god casting a shadow in our faces, as it was shaded by the native lantern ; what wonder if sleep with its welcome quiet refused to close our eyes until the wee small hours?

The story and legend of this beautiful island, which I had heard in the evening, crowded upon my mind, and the remembrance of it has never been effaced.

What wonder if the legends now told, and by the Japanese believed, that this picturesque isle rose out of the sea, crowned by the goddess " Benten the Beautiful " seemed almost a truth? To me it seems no wonder, where so much of the beautiful is woven with the tales of this wonderful land, that the very children imbibe it as a sacred story and refuse to disbelieve. In later days as many as three priests claim to have enjoyed the sight of this august goddess, Benten —the patroness of lovely Enoshima.

One of them was thus addressed by her: " All the world is my possession ; all people my children." It is said that a nobleman, Tokimaka, came here to pray for the prosperity of his family. After long prayers, continued for many days, Benten appeared to him and told him his prayers were remembered by her, and promised him a blessing. She then vanished into the sea, showing her real body, which was that of a dragon.

Tokimaka saw some bright objects sparkling on the ground, which proved to be three scales from the body of the dragon goddess. On picking them up they arranged themselves into the form of a crest, and this trefoil of dragon scales became the crest and monogram of the Hojo family, to which dignity Tokimaka soon arrived.

All over Japan there are numerous shrines and temples to commemorate her memory. This island, which is dedicated to Benten, contains four temples, in all of which she is pictured mild

and motherly, wearing a crown containing a
torii (gateway) and by her side a huge dragon.

In the morning we were awakened by the
smart clapping of hands from the room of our
guide, that being the manner of calling the servants, as no bells are used in Japanese inns.
Soon we were dressed and enjoyed a run down
the steep street, after which we partook of a
Japanese breakfast, helped out with eggs and
a cup of coffee.

After securing an old native to show us the
way about the island, we started for the top of
the eminence, where we hoped to make a more
intimate acquaintance with her saintship Benten.
We toiled up many steps and at last arrived at
the first Benten, where "we paid the dimes (two)
and in we went," as we did at all four of the
shrines, until we finally reached the top, out of
breath and rather disgusted with Bentens, which
were little more than temples by name, and not
one causing a feeling of delight. The most
noticeable thing about them was a strong fishy
smell, caused no doubt by the food upon which
this ancient goddess is fed.

From the summit we had a grand view of the
ocean, and from a tall tree that sheltered the
fourth Benten "a giant eagle, perched on high,
with wings outspread looked down."

Now came the descent to the caves, which we
reached in safety. The tide being high we were
compelled to go by an artificial road built with
bamboo up against the rocks, out of reach of the
swelling ocean. At the mouth we were met by
a priest with his lighted tapers, ready to guide us
to the interior, and whose services we were glad
to employ. On we followed until the further
end was reached, which was blocked by a shrine,
where a shaven headed priest stood ready to sell
us one prayer or many, which blessing could be

obtained for a few cents, and if we may believe our interpreter, it was all that was required to waft us on a lotus leaf to the Buddhists' Paradise.

The original shrine of Benten was formerly kept here, and on certain days, many priests and worshipers resorted to the cave and removed the goddess to air it, and then returned it to the corner in this cavern, with much ceremony. Tradition records the caves as the dwelling place of two white dragons, probably little Bentens.

It is said that in times past, the passage led through under the sea to the main land, but has at the present time been closed to prevent accident. The galleries in the rocks have in many places been marred by pick and ax by the Japanese while searching for gold. In our wanderings about we were soon lost and were glad to call lustily for our priestly guide, whom we soon saw approaching from an unexpected direction, following the twinkling of his little light. The sensation during our exploration was agreeable and satisfactory, although wild and weird in the extreme, but when we had once emerged into the bright sunlight, a shudder as if we had just escaped from a tomb passed over us, and all were thankful to see and feel the light of day.

On our way back, another of the attractions of the place was witnessed, which was diving from the highest rocks into the sea. These divers were very expert and rarely failed to bring up a shell from the deep. The act was more to be deplored than applauded, for it was painful to see the poor creatures shivering with the cold of winter and begging for a penny after each performance. Tired out with our tramp we slowly wended our way back to the hotel, where we found our jinrikisha men from the station waiting to take us back to the cars, to which we were soon on our way.

When we gathered up our clothing and curios we had picked up and bought, we found a large addition to our packages, which when we came to examine was found to be all the unbroken food left from the three meals of which we had partaken at the hotel, it being the custom of the Japanese to take all the food they cannot eat when dining at any place, and they were pleased to place us under the same rule as they did their own countrymen ; but, under the circumstances, we did not wish to accept the benefit of their generosity.

After passing over the miraculously raised sand beach connecting this beautiful island to the main land, we drove through the little village of Katase, famous, or rather infamous, for its uncleanliness and fishy smells, its uninviting tea houses and its insignificant Buddhist temple, and were soon out into the country, where we could admire the beautiful surroundings made by nature's hand, but adorned by the labor of this ingenious people. The many fine groves and tiny lakes, the gardens turned to beds and walks in which some of the more hardy shrubs and flowers were beginning to show their green as an advance guard, were sufficient indications of the beauties yet to be.

On we went at a good, round trot, as the roads were level and our human teams, like country horses, knew that home and rest were ahead, so that we soon dashed up to the station at Fujisawa. This little town contains an old temple of a peculiar sect of Buddhists, and the cemetery is quite noted as the burial place of many members of the Hojo family. The name of town and station interpreted means wisteria meadow, and it abounds with that vine in every place where the hand of cultivation has not made a more necessary use of the soil. Some fine old Icho trees are about the station and temple, several of which are said to have passed the age of five hundred years.

After a cup of tea at the station tea house, the whistle of the engine caused us to gather up our packages and hasten to take a seat in the rolling carriage that was to carry us home. On our way near the station Totska, which we passed, are some artificial caves, the walls being covered with representations of various real and imaginary creatures.

It is said they are well worth a visit, but time was short, the train in a hurry, so on we went leaving them behind. Shortly after we swept into Yokohama, and although so far from our native land, rejoiced that we had arrived at our temporary home.

CHAPTER V.

AFTER a few days of rest our Princess, Kuma, was requested to make one of a party to the city of Tokio, which request was graciously complied with, so one fine morning found us all at the Yokohama station, where we took the train for the capital city, some eighteen miles distant. In a few moments after leaving the station the country is gained, and you are at once in rural Japan, which is even more charming than the city.

A few miles out of Yokohama we passed a number of extensive shell mounds, which were first discovered when the railroad was being constructed. They are similar to those found in Maine and Florida, but lack the stone implements, either arrows, spear heads or other flint utensils which are found so plentifully in those mounds in the States.

Vast quantities of pottery of many shapes and different ornamentations from those now manufactured, were found in the heaps. Strange, that like the West, this land has its unknown and unreadable monuments of a lost race. The road leads through a volcanic country, the mountains of which are covered with shrubs and trees.

The plains are mostly devoted to rice culture, which is the Japanese staple food. The people are generally poor. The smallness of landholdings is said to be the main cause among the agricultural class. If it is a source of poverty, it is also an incentive to contrivance and industry, and shows what can be done on a piece of land not much larger than a house lot in America.

The proprietors will throw up ranges of miniature hills, trace winding paths about their base and to their summit, suggest beetling crags, purling streams, and silvery cascades by artistically selecting and arranging stones, and then give life to the scene by wonderful evergreens, gnarled and knotted trees, with here and there patches of brilliant golden and crimson flowers springing up, as it were, to brighten the tiny landscape at the right season of the year.

The villages are bright, with scrupulously neat and clean houses, each with its attached garden, and often a tiny pond of gold and silver fish, while the whole is made gay with gaudy flags and brilliant lanterns.

Early in the forenoon we arrived at the traveler's Mecca, the city of Tokio, the capital of this Island Empire.

Our guide soon engaged jinrikishas and men to take us about to see the wonders in the chief city of this eastern land. The city, which is over nine miles in length and eight in breadth, is built on an immense plain, so that the eye could at a glance survey the whole space if the vision would permit, and at every turn there would open to view new features in landscape, water, castles and massive edifices with which this prairie city of the Flowery land, is everywhere studded.

Although so much has been written about this Yedo of the past, it is in reality not an ancient city, but can claim an antiquity dating back no further than 1600, when it contained only one small castle surrounded by a few scattering villages spread about upon its flat, even surface.

These were inhabited by farmers and fishermen, whose produce and catch were conveyed into the interior for sale.

In 1604 it began to gain prominence, as at that date the first Shogun (Prince) of the Tokugawa family made it his capital. His successor was his grandson, the noted Iyemitsu, who greatly improved the place and set in motion the ball which rolled on until Tokio became the largest and most populous city of this eastern kingdom. In 1868 the rule of the Shogunate was overthrown, and it then became the capital of the whole Empire. This plain was formerly called Kwanto, meaning eastern barrier, and it was here that the troops of many different rulers were mustered, drilled and stationed, during their reign, to prevent the hordes of eastern people from spreading over this portion of Japan, as each Daimio or petty ruler was very jealous of any encroachment upon his territory or rights.

But while I have been learning the early history of Japan, or rather Tokio, our jinrikisha men have brought us to the foot of a long flight of stone steps, leading to the summit of Atago Yama, a noted eminence near the temple Shiba.

The flight of steps leading straight to the top is chosen, and we commence the ascent of the many hundred, which are so nearly perpendicular that a small chain secured to iron posts in the granite is gladly caught hold of to help us up this steep incline. As we sink into a seat when once we have scaled the summit, and cast our eyes about, we feel well repaid for the trouble and toil as in silence we gaze at the wonderful panorama which lies in beauty in and about the vast plain beneath.

Here we found the ubiquitous tea house girls, who quickly relieved our fatigue by a cup of refreshing tea, in which was an infusion of salted cherry blossoms, much more refreshing than palatable. Etiquette requires you to take the cup whether you drink the contents or not.

Towards the bay is a magnificent view of the forts, warships, and numerous fishing craft plying in and out of the many creeks, while to the south is the fishermen's city, called Shinagawa, where thousands of excursionists go to gather shell fish and oysters, which are plentiful on the long stretch of beach uncovered at low tide.

The streets are lined with maple trees, making a bright green line among the brown straw-roofed huts. From the western side, a view of the Hakone mountains can be obtained, while in majesty above them rises sacred Fusi Yama, the pride of Japan. The trees about Ueno park show like a forest in the middle of this sea of houses, and mark the plain with an additional beauty. From here the royal residence and castle is seen very plainly. To the northwest is the section of the city called Tskiji, which includes the foreign settlement of Tokio.

The engineering college and the buildings of the foreign legation rise grandly above those of the natives, among which they are built, that of the Russians being of such size and height as to show all over the city.

On the extreme top of this mount is a Shinto shrine containing a god, supposed to protect against fire. Carved on stone and under the same roof, are representations of the Goddess Benten (of beauty), the gods Ebisu (of happiness) and Daikoku (of wealth), the work being well executed. The 24th of each month the people take as a day for recreation, when they visit this shrine to admire the scenery and worship in the temple.

As one gazes upon the city below, he is struck by the many small rivers, wide canals, and moats winding about in all parts and in all directions.

Flocks of wild ducks and other birds could be seen gliding about the canals or flying over head, seemingly unconscious of the thousands of people who lined the banks. Fish are said to be abundant in the moats and streams, but as the people are not allowed to catch them, or to shoot the birds, they are of no benefit.

We gave a few cents to the tea house girls, or attendants, and as many more to the presiding god of the temple, when we descended from our elevation by another flight of steps winding about the cliffs so that the ascent or descent is much easier, and is used for old men and women; we found we had become quite old enough to take advantage of them.

From the street we followed our guide to the celebrated Ko Yo Kwan, Ko Yo, meaning red maple leaves, and Kwan (pronounced *can*) a building or club house owned by the nobles of Tokio. It consists of two modern buildings, which are situated on the top of a hill and surrounded by pretty walks and plots of flowers tastefully and artistically laid out; all this cannot fail to attract many visitors where they all seem to admire the beautiful so much. The first building we entered was used as a tea and lunch house of the first class, and patronized only by the nobles of the highest order.

Everything in the building, which contained many rooms, was decorated with maple leaves in the different stages of their coloring, but most of them were in the color of those beautified by the first frosts of autumn. The ceiling overhead as well as the sides, the thick mats at our feet, the doors, panels, and paper windows, the brasier of coals, the cups for tea, and the trays on which the cups were passed, the tea-pot and tea canister, the musical instruments and articles of amusement, as well as the dresses of the attendants were decorated with the maple leaf, of so elegant a design, that one could not help thinking of the beauties of our northern home, when our forests are resplendent with the beautiful foliage of this tree.

Crossing a garden of flowers which separates the two buildings, we entered the second, which is devoted to the performance of Japanese operatic music, and the celebrated " No " dance, illustrating an ancient legend of the customs of the Japanese people. The stage is very plain, but no doubt suitable for the performances.

Under the boards of the stage are placed huge earthenware vases, from which a peculiar sound issues as the floor is stamped upon, it being both curious and pleasing. The walls, which are ceiled with wide boards, are ornamented with paintings, chiefly representations of pine trees, storks, and flying cranes. Here the Mikado often comes to witness a new play, and we were allowed to draw apart the curtain and gaze at the divan of His Imperial Highness, and all the paraphernalia of his private box.

The whole, which was neat and comfortable, was modest and inexpensive, not at all as one would suppose or expect to find any place ever honored by an Eastern Potentate. The rooms were cared for by a young lady of the nobility, but who did not let the dignity of high birth overcome her ideas of ladyship, as she was gracious and attentive in all her manners. On leaving the place we were offered a cup of tea, and accompanying sweetmeats, and given a card upon which a cluster of maple leaves was printed in colors, as a reminder of our visit.

From the club house we directed our steps to Shiba, which is well called the " Garden of Tokio." Pretty gardens full of flowers and evergreens are seen in all directions. The roads, which are wide and clean, are planted on both sides with massive evergreen trees affording a delightful shade. At every turn, priests in their sacerdotal robes, and with shaven heads, are met, who gladly avail themselves of a chance to earn a penny by showing you about the temple grounds, and the tombs of the illustrious Shoguns, which are noted for the magnificence and richness displayed in their architecture.

The grounds are very extensive, containing many acres. It must be remembered that a Japanese temple is not one compact building, but consists of many separate ones within a compound or garden. The Shiba temple comprises many parts, each governed by different priests and entirely distinct from the others, except that they are contained in one enclosure, dedicated to Shiba. The principal building is usually larger than the others and more elaborately finished.

The people resort to these grounds as much or more to enjoy the beauties of place and scenery, meet old friends, and chat or gossip, as they do to worship.

In every private house the family has a shrine with one or more gods enclosed, where they can worship any time they wish ; besides, they have a temple near their residence to which they often resort, and which they support by their purse and presence, much as we sustain our clergy in America.

The Japs being a jovial, pleasure seeking people, visit the noted temples as a pastime, in families and groups, the same as we visit noted places of amusement, or to hear some celebrated lecturer, except that they take along food for the day, and have a good time feasting with the gods, and to which feast they feel highly honored, if one of the priests will deign to partake.

The most celebrated of the Shiba temples is

Zojoji, in and about which lies buried seven of their Shoguns or ancient rulers. We first entered a pebbled court leading directly to the front of this edifice. On each side are arranged two hundred stone lanterns, standing about eight feet high, cut from solid granite, on the top of which is a square cap containing four windows into which, from the top, on festival nights, a torch is placed and must make the whole surroundings beautiful. These are all offerings to the deceased friends of the petty rulers or daimios. Those of a higher grade have presented numerous and elegant bronze lanterns by their friends, to light them to the Buddhists' Paradise. We passed through the main temple, around which ran a grand corridor, along which, at certain hours of the day, some of the principal idols are carried.

If it is on the occasion of a national or sacred festival, the idols are preceded by a procession of flowers carried by church devotees, the advance always carrying plum blossoms followed in regular order by the cherry, the wisteria, the iris, and ending with the chrysanthemum. We viewed with pleasure the ornamental ceilings and artistically wrought panels, and the wonderful carvings in wood, bronze and stone; gazed into the room where the sacred urns and other utensils under priestly care were deposited, but which, not having had time to examine, we must leave for some writer better qualified in ghostly lore, to describe.

We were soon at the tomb of the sixth Shogun, who was one of the last of the Shogunate of note, and were surprised at the amount of wealth in bronze, marble, silver and gold, with which his resting place was decorated. All the old legends of the East, that I have ever read, were in my mind as the guide hurried us on to the tomb of the second ruler who was ever buried there, and who so honored his wife as to allow her remains to repose by his side. For a time we were filled with surprise and wonder at the magnificence and expense which was so lavishly employed in the embellishment of the tomb of this royal pair. The sacred urns standing many feet high, were of solid bronze and copper, very massive and ornamented with plates of pure gold and silver.

As no temple of importance exists that has not several gates of different forms and designs, with generally a name referring to its form, or some beautiful carved work, the entrance to this place was no exception. The front of this mausoleum was guarded by a pair of solid bronze gates, very massive, and hung to two huge posts of bronze, which were crossed high up by a large bronze beam forming a gateway or *torii*, through which we passed after the gates were unlocked by our attendant priests. They were so heavy that it required two persons to start them open, and when once in motion they swung with resistless force against their guards. About this tomb were arranged many shrines and lanterns, all rich in carving and material. If it took all the strength of Samson to remove the gates of Gaza in Bible days, one of our party concluded he would have had to grow in strength until the present time to be able to remove the guard gates from this burial place. Tradition states that these two gates came from Corea, which seems to be the source of many a Japanese treasure. The inside of one of the minor temples has a rich paneled ceiling, carved and colored, while paintings of flowers, birds, dragons and clouds, are lavishly disposed on the upper portion of the building. Bronze is the favorite material used, and judges of the work say that for delicacy and sharpness of the reliefs cast upon its surface, it is unsurpassed by any metal work in the world.

In the front of Monolith Lavatory (so called), we were shown a large granite urn, with a mouth over two feet across, gradually growing less until at the depth of three feet the excavation ended. This was partly full of water, and we were told by our guide (in all sincerity) that it was full twice in twenty-four hours, and that the miracle was caused by the prayer of an old priest who wished a token from Buddha of his acceptance into the divine paradise.

I wished to examine the boulder on which it sat to see where the pipe which helped perform the miracle entered the vase, but was gently reminded by the priest that it was time to be on the move.

CHAPTER VI.

FEELING that we had visited the places of
greatest interest, we turned our human teams
towards a hotel, on our way passing by the Shiro
or imperial castle with its massive wall and
tower, its huge gateways and deep moats, not
only obtaining a fine view of the same, but also
of a large portion of the city. The gardens within the castle enclosure were prettily laid out,
and many foreign fruits and flowers were cultivated in abundance.

The Tokio house was soon reached where,
after a refreshing meal, excellently cooked and
well served, we again loaded our carriages, put
spurs to our steeds, and rolled along to the
Shinto temple, which was erected in memory of
the soldiers of the Imperial Army, who were
slain in different wars for the defence of the
Mikado.

Adjoining this temple is the Tokio race-course,
and a park, both favorite lounging places where
many Japanese resort to witness fireworks, which
they manufacture and exhibit to perfection. At
the end of the course nearest to the temple, is a
huge stone tower with an iron cage on the top, in
which, at night, a light is continually kept, in
honor of the soldiers buried there. The wide

level street leading to this temple was some eighty rods in length, and on both sides were booths, stalls, and open plots of ground covered with articles for sale, consisting of the useful, ornamental, and curious. Some crystals from the interior were very large, and almost as transparent as diamonds.

The entrance to this temple was between two immense composition pillars, crossed by a large beam of the same forming the *torii*, so sacred to the Japanese, which were cast from the brass and iron cannon captured by the government soldiers during many wars. They were the most massive of anything in mixed metals, seen in Japan, and must be of great weight and value. After a hasty examination of this temple we passed through into the street which passed the castle, and took another look at the palace, which seemed to be composed of several different styles of architecture, part of it appearing very ancient and other parts looking as if it had just escaped from the hands of an American builder. . A portion of it (one wing) is said to be used as a place of entertainment for distinguished foreign guests. We crossed the *Bashi* (bridge), where a regent of Japan was assassinated as late as 1860 by the "ronins" of the daimio of this district. These sixteen ronins (wanderers) without a master, planned to present a petition as the palanquin passed, a common practice at that time. The escort scarcely noticed them until they struck down the palanquin bearers. Before they could rally to the Regent's rescue his head had been cut off and all but four of the murderers escaped. A letter found on the body of one left dead on the bridge, gave as a reason for the deed, that he was too   in his manners with foreigners and too willing to conclude treaties with western barbarians.

Night found us all gathered at the hotel, where we were alloted rooms large and commodious, containing good clean European beds, and what was most enjoyable of all was a hot coal fire built in an American stove, which dispensed its warmth about us, and was a fitting and grateful close to a happy day.

As we gazed the next morn from our windows, a cold dull sky, with now and again a spit of snow, seemed to tell us that our sight seeing for the day would be spoiled, but our little Princess seeing the looks of disappointment on our faces said in her naïve way "no can snow, sun by and by shine, we go all same." Sure enough the sun did shine, for by nine o'clock the sky was bright and clear, and our spirits rose with that orb of light, as we glided over the smooth street, in our two wheeled carriage, on our way to visit the most beautiful park in all Japan, Ueno.

This place is celebrated for its fine temples and beautiful grounds, and also as the burial place of six of the ancient Shoguns or Tycoons, and for that reason is called the twin of Shiba temple. In former times a relative of the Mikado, called Miya (Prince), resided here and exercised his authority as prime ruler of the eastern portion of the city. In 1868, a battle was fought in this park, resulting in a victory for the government, and secured to the Mikado the permanency of his reign. The entrance, as is usual in this country, is up a wide, handsome street, through a large gate, and then up a flight of stone steps where you can overlook a part of the city and see in the distance the surrounding mountains.

Again we were assailed by the tea house girls, with their red lips and quaint attire, who offered us sweets and tea and were much disappointed by a refusal to partake.

Here an enterprising Japanese has a fine hotel

conducted on the European plan, where the best
of the land is provided for the guests.   The gardens about the house are artistically laid out, and
the hungry traveler could not find a prettier
place to dine and at the same time admire the
gorgeous scenery.   Near the hotel is a bronze
image, filled with clay, twenty-two feet high,
representing Great Buddha, the Japanese Dai
Butsu.   This idol, worshiped by many of the
people, is called the Light of God, and is covered
by a small temple roof painted red, easy of access
to all who wish to examine it or worship at the
shrine.

On the outskirts of the Park is a small lake full
of the lotus, which are in bloom in early August,
and are said to be of an exceedingly beautiful
form and graceful elegance.   Also connected
with the place is a Zoological garden, containing
a few beasts and many birds.   Among the rest
are many rare domestic fowl, some of a singular
species.   One lot of hens was of a pure white
plumage, but instead of feathers on back and
breast, were covered with a long white substance resembling hair.   Another lot of fowl had
tail feathers of remarkable length ; one cock was
proudly strutting about whose tail feathers, three
in number, were each sixteen feet long.   They
were cared for by experts, as the species is nearly
extinct.   I hope the reader will believe that I
tell him truthfully, that the long feathers were
curled and put in papers each night, as carefully
as a young lady would crimp her hair for the
coming next day's fair.   There were many other
beautiful birds with brilliant plumage ; among
them the golden pheasant, a native of Japan, was
conspicuous.

This portion of the grounds is beautiful in
May, when the forests of cherry trees, with
which it is set, are in full bloom.   In another

part of the park is a large building of modern construction used for a school, and also open as an exhibition. Here could be seen everything manufactured by the Japanese, from ancient periods until the present time, showing what advance and improvement they had made in tools, carpentry, machinery, clothing material, and also in what labors they had ever engaged, such as fishing, farming and shipping.

By the side of implements of all trades, were much and various machinery, and models employed in different works, made by the most ingenious of American and European nations.

By the side of the American sewing machine of the most improved pattern, were the fish bone needles of Japan, as well as their steel needles, more modern, but rough and unpolished. There was the rude Japanese lantern and torch light contrasting with an American chandelier; a model of one of the Cape Ann fishing craft, with her fine lines and symmetrically shaped hull and tapering spars, by the side of the Eastern junk. All was interesting, the contrast between the past and the present being more than it was possible to attempt to realize.

We found ourselves asking the question, Will the next few hundred years make as much change for the better? Will it be possible, or shall we go back and adopt the past, its manners, works and fashions?

From this building, a few rods east led us to another park enclosed within the main one where the grand museum of Japan is collected. Here could be seen everything for which this wonderful country is noted, from the Mikado's crown, to the peasant's wooden clog, from the gilded palanquin and trappings of State to the hut of the poorest and most degraded of the nation. The diamond hilted sword was here, as well as the people's stone knives and hatchets with which in the interior they still till and cultivate the ground. Here in profusion is the elegant porcelain ware from Satsuma, Hizen and Kaga, with the beautiful Cloisonne of Kiota and the magnificent lacquer ware of Hakodate. About this park I will not tire my readers more, if I am fortunate enough to have any, but will follow our guide to Asakusa Park, there to admire the beauties of this interesting vicinity.

Asakusa is the name of a district or portion of Tokio in which are the extensively laid out grounds of a beautiful park or common, and centered in the same is a popular, and by many called the most celebrated temple in Japan. This temple in the general way of speaking is called Asakusa, but its proper name is Kin Ryu Zan. It is dedicated to the Shinto religion, the old worship of the nation, but particularly to the Goddess Kwanon Sama. Visitors of this sect and worshipers of this merciful goddess rush to see a representation of the miracles wrought in answer to prayer, which to them excel everything else. The tableau consists of over thirty life size wax figures, which are so very suggestive as to be understood with but little explanation. The main entrance to the temple is up a long lane paved with stone, both sides of which are lined with shops of moderate height, all in one long brick building, which was divided into rooms, some ten by twelve feet each, very gayly decorated and full of toys and ornaments to keep as curios or as a propitiatory offering to the many gods in the enclosure. At the gateway are two buildings painted red, one on either side, each containing a god of huge proportions, standing in niches and protected by iron gratings or screens. These are the guardians of the gate and temple and the outer sentinel of the grounds.

They are supposed to represent "Two Kings."
One stands ready to welcome those who repent
of their sins and determine to lead new lives,
while the other welcomes the birth of an infant
destined to become a good man.

As one passes through he is met by flocks of
tame pigeons, which are all about and are held
sacred by the people.

Women are round the temple front, selling
peas and rice in little earthern pots, so as to give
people a chance to feed them, that being one
way to gain the good will of this venerable goddess.

As the Japanese do not visit this place from
pious motives altogether, but as a pleasure resort,
one will find for their amusement in the grounds,
a theatre, circus, archery galleries, tea booths
and shops, besides various other minor exhibi-
tions.

There are many other subordinate temples
with shrines and images as well as other attractions to invite the curiosity of the traveler. One
building of octagonal form contains many hundred idols. There is also a tall pagoda temple
with its five alternate roofs one above the other.
This in its bright red paint and dazzling gilt
roofs is seen from afar, and is a thing to be
noticed at once the garden is reached.

In the main temple building there is an audience hall, and back of the sacred symbols a large
hall for the performance of religious dances and
other sacred rites. In the most sacred part of
the temple, where it can only be seen by the
priests, except upon certain occasions, is kept a
little image some two inches in height and nearly
as broad. It is made of solid gold, and repre-
sents the goddess and patroness of the temple,
Kwanon.

These are all within the Asakusa grounds, and

it will take an hour or two to give them a passing
examination. It also affords an interesting picture of native outdoor life. Near this park, and
really an attraction of the same, an enterprising
Jap has erected a miniature tower, some two
hundred feet high, to resemble Fusi Yama, and it
is called by that name by the people of Tokio.
Steps lead up around the outside, which gives so
gradual an ascent that it is not tiresome. The
whole is made of bamboo, the lower part covered
with plaster and then painted in colors to resemble the rough stone of different kinds, native
to Japan. The top is much the same except
that it is white, with a wash to resemble the
snow with which the real Fusi is almost always
crowned. The builder was fortunate in his enter-
prise, as it was stated by the local papers that
during the first nine days, more than a quarter of
a million of people visited the top, the entrance
fees amounting to some ten thousand "yens"
(dollars).

From the top nothing could be seen except
the ocean or bay on one side, and the large flat
city, with its long, wavy lines of huts, trees, and
temples in every other direction, with a dark
background of distant mountains. The day
was bright, the atmosphere clear, but for all that
the eye could not pierce to the outside of the
vast sea of human homes.

The immensity of this mighty city was beyond
conception when viewed from such a place.

It looked like the ocean when one is at sea, and
the sun is disappearing beneath the horizon and
the space about us is the whole world; but instead of water, this was one great sea of habita-
tions, too great to enumerate.

Near this artificial mount were long galleries
of wax works, statues, and a long row of marine
caves in which were exhibited many rare marine

productions, among which fish of beautiful colors were sporting. Here we rested in the " rich man's " garden, with its miniature hills, rustic bowers, artificial water courses, and loung- ing places where people can rest, sup the tea of Japan, inhale the fragrance of flowers, and con- template the pretty landscape.

After we had rested sufficiently, we proceeded to an Asakusa eating house, winding through many crooked streets and grim lanes until at last we emerged into an opening in the middle of the city, containing more than half an acre, where we found a pretty little cottage, sur- rounded by everything with which the Japanese beautify their homes. We were soon at the little table, a brasier of coals on each side of us, and a dinner before us which an epicure could not re- sist, especially if he was waited upon as we were, by the beautiful O-Kiku-San (chrysanthemum).

To follow out our well matured plans, we once more took our jinrikishas, or rather they took us, to the banks of the Sumida Gawa, where we em- barked, carriages and all, in long flat boats, for the opposite side, the quiet and picturesque island of Mukojima. One can imagine something of the size of this great city when he thinks of the wide river flowing through it, in which there is an island over four miles long and nearly half as wide, on which there live over thirty thousand inhabitants.

This island, which is really an enormous park and pleasure ground, is noted for its plum and cherry forests, and is visited by the people from all parts of Japan, at the season they are in bloom. In the enclosure among the winding paths are many tea houses and shrines, also large stones set in the by-paths, and on them the name of some founder of this, or some other public resort, engraved, and the merit of the gift expatiated upon. Near the entrance is a small pottery, where the people make a cheap porcelain on which they paint the plum or cherry blossom, and which you can see moulded, painted and baked, if you care to wait. These can be purchased for a small sum if you wish mementos of the place. One of the most singular freaks of nature, and worthy of note is, that although throughout the city and country the plum and cherry trees are in great profusion, the perfumes of the blossoms are floating in every space, and the trees even are held in almost devotional reverence, yet they are only a tree of deceit. They were never known to bear a single cherry or plum ; and the foreigner from America who thinks of the delicious cherries of our country, is disappointed when he sees the white and pink blossoms covering the distant fields like snow and is told that there never was a plum or cherry raised on a native tree in Japan. Attempts have been made to introduce the cherry tree from San Francisco, but have been attended with little success.

On our return to the city we rode to the south end of the island, crossed the river by the famous bridge, Nihon Bashi, which led us into the center of the metropolis. At the south end of the bridge still hung the government notice boards, now of little use, as the printing press has supplied their place by its more powerful method of disseminating its news. On these boards, as late as 1868, edicts against Christianity were posted.

The ladies of our party returned to the hotel to rest, so we drove to the most distant part of the city to visit a place where Japanese girls are bought and sold. In reality, it is a regular exchange, where people could be disposed of to agents for certain sums, for almost any length of time, from a month to years.

It is no uncommon thing for women to dispose of themselves to raise money to give a loved parent a grand funeral, and they often put themselves into a broker's hands to be sold as advantageously as possible, in order to raise the sum required for that purpose. Here we were indeed surprised, for it was not only a reminder of the slave marts the writer once visited near Richmond, Va., but it also reminded him of the degradation to which an intelligent community must be reduced to allow such a trade and traffic in their very midst. There were long rows of buildings as fine as any in Tokio, crowded full of girls and women from ten to forty years of age, and there must have been at least a thousand, as the houses for more than a mile on each side of the street were full. With a sensation, which for the first time crept into my mind, that all Japan was not a paradise, we turned our men towards the railroad station with heavy hearts, caused by the misery and degradation we had come so far to witness.

We soon crossed another bridge and were at once rolled in to the new Boulevard, called Ginza, which terminates at the station of Shimbashi. This street is the grandest in Tokio, being four miles long, ninety feet wide, and as straight as an arrow. The center is macadamized, the sidewalks wide, and laid with brick. The houses on each side are two and three stories high, substantially built, and of both European and Japanese designs. Along the sides are rows of trees near together, affording a shade for the thousands who are continually moving along its way.

The shops are tastefully arranged and make an imposing show. As the noise of a horn sounded behind us, we turned to look, and saw dashing along to the station, an American horse-car with its four horses attached, and as it passed, the words Newark and New Jersey were distinctly seen on the front. So it was at almost every place; there would be some reminder of our own loved land, even if nothing more than a case of oil brought by our own ship to this "Land of the East."

The station is reached, our guide had tickets secured as well as a car section for our own use, and which we were glad to avail ourselves of, as the Japanese fill every car they occupy with smoke. In a few moments we were in motion, driving on our way to Yokohama, our temporary home.

CHAPTER VII.

YOKOHAMA, Feb. 9, '89.

DEAR SIR, CAPTAIN,

I thank you heartily for your kind visit to me here. I have to spare the day when will you leave this country, because I not see you long.

I beg to add few more about the declaration of our constitutional law. This 11th shall indeed be happy day that would forever be remembered. On this date the public citizen will receive His Majesty in the " voice of happiness," and the people of the neighboring districts will crowd to the city. Here and there, shows, curious, theatres, and all kinds of games will cover all parts of the metropolice. You come my house, therefore, 9 ohayo (morning), with Okamisan (Madam), also Gracesan (Miss Grace).

Yours faithfully,

Y. TOYONAGA.

Of course the morning of the 11th found us all at our friend's house, and as soon as we had removed our shoes, we were ushered into the presence of Princess Kuma, who gave us a kindly welcome and seated us upon the floor on silk-covered mats or cushions with which all Japanese houses are plentifully supplied.

The rooms were devoid of furniture, unless we except a large chest of drawers in one end, in which during the day are kept the bedding used at night, as well as the cushions and prayer mats not in use. In the center of each room, there being three, was the usual square box, filled with sand (called hibachi), on which they kept a charcoal fire, both for warmth and for heating tea, which is always ready to be served. In one corner was hung a silk screen or banner covered with large Japanese characters and figures, while in front of the same was a little altar on top of which was an ill-shaped-faced god. In front of this was a collation mixed with many curious articles of both Japanese and foreign art. This was the household altar and place of meditation and prayer.

Usually at night one or more wax candles are burned in its front. The floor was covered with mats of the finest rice straw, bleached to snowy whiteness. Over the door was hung the long sword of the deceased father (a daimio), and during our stay we were shown the short sword, which was kept in a separate apartment ; people of this rank were entitled to wear two. The hilt was richly adorned, as was also the regalia, which we were allowed to examine.

The slight framework, which runs in grooves was shoved aside, making the three rooms one, into which was brought a square table not over six inches high, covered with a silk cloth, on which was placed a lunch of cakes, sweets, nuts and oranges ; the tea was made and turned by our friend, Toyonaga, the smallest cups filled for us ; the smaller the cup the greater honor. We all gathered around the board, and had a joyful time with our mingling of English, Spanish and Japanese.

As soon as the hospitalities were over we found jinrikishas had been ordered for us, and so we started, a merry party of five, to see the display, and help by our presence to usher in the new Constitution which would bring this " Land of the East " into closer bonds of fraternity with the powers of the West.

As we left the house we were surprised at the number of Japanese flags that had been placed about the dwelling after we had entered, and what was most gratifying was to see our own dear American banner entwined with that of Japan, over the gateway leading to our friend's abode. Under the eaves were many little bells to which were fastened paper prayers. The wind blowing them about gave a sweet, musical sound, and this was one way to waft their prayers to the great God above, as well as through the intercession of the numerous gods below.

A word about this same constitution before I attempt to describe the wonders seen during this great national event, which occupied one day in proclaiming, and two additional in rejoicing.

At 10 A. M., February 11th, 1889, the Emperor, in presence of his cabinet, in the Imperial Sanctuary at Tokio, took an oath to maintain and secure from decline the ancient form of government, and at all times by example, show to his subjects his willingness to abide by, and execute all laws; then took his place upon the Imperial throne, from which he handed to the President of State, "The Constitution of Japan," the "Imperial Ordinance of the House of Peers," the "Law of the Houses," the "Law of Election of Members of the House of Representatives," and the "Law of Finance;" as before, the Mikado remains the source of the law, exercised with the sanction of the two Houses or Diet.

To himself, the issuing of all ordinances to carry out the Laws as well as for the maintenance of peace and order are delegated. He also has supreme command of the Army and Navy, the power to declare war or make peace, as well as treaties, confer rank, titles and other marks of honor. Also to grant pardons and commute punishments.

The House of Peers and the House of Representatives constitute the Imperial Diet. The Upper House is partly elective, partly hereditary, and partly nominated. The elective portion comprises both noblemen and commoners.

The first are Counts, Viscounts, and Barons, and are elected by the members of their representative orders, the number elected never to exceed one fifth of the number of each order. The commoners are chosen by cities and districts, one member from each, and are to be taken from among the highest tax payers, and after their election must be approved by the Emperor; if not, then it is to no effect.

The nominated portion comprises persons nominated by his Majesty on account of service to the State, or of erudition. These are life members; the elected members sit seven years, which is the term of the Upper House. It is also laid down that the number of Imperial nominees, together with those elected, shall not exceed the number of nobles in the House. The hereditary part consists of members of the Imperial family, Princes and Marquises.

The Lower House consists of three hundred members elected by ballot from districts fixed by law. All candidates are to be thirty years of age, and shall have paid a national tax of at least fifteen dollars, the previous year. A member sits for four years, and each elected member of the Lower House, as well as each elected, or nominated, member of the Upper House, receives eight hundred yens per year, and traveling expenses.

Persons upon whom suffrage is conferred must be twenty-five years of age, and subject to have paid the same amount of tax as the least sum (fifteen yens) which is required to make the candidate eligible. On the whole, it seems but little the people have gained, but it is a beginning, and what gives the most satisfaction to the people is that a little liberty is granted, and this has been done by the Mikado's own free will; and his willingness to do the best possible, and giving up the least power for his subjects' good has touched a tender chord in every one's heart, and has placed this throne more securely in the hearts of his people than ever it was when his rule was the most sanguine or most despotic.

The dress of the Mikado on this occasion was of Western fashion, now adopted as the dress of State.

Great preparations were made all over the country to have the ceremony imposing and ostentatious. At Tokio, only nine foreigners outside the Legations could obtain permission to be present at the Declaration, as it was intended to be a national act, not an international one.

The members of the Imperial Cabinet, including the Princes and Princesses, gave a banquet at the Palace during the evening to which were invited all the Diplomatic Corps. At the barracks the soldiers were entertained. Thirty cows and fifty-eight pigs served as a foundation for their feasts.

The gates of the prisons throughout Japan were thrown open and more than two thousand prisoners were welcomed again to freedom. Large sums of money were donated to every object of good, one man in Tokio giving ten thousand dollars to be distributed among the poor of his neighborhood.

All Japanese Ministers abroad were ordered by the Foreign office to give elaborate entertainments to their respective Legations.

The Navy was well represented at Yokohama

and at 10 A. M. rolled out a national salute,
which was answered by the guns from the warships of not less than six nations. In the foreign
settlement at Yokohama the business places were
closed, and nearly all of them were decorated
with arches of evergreens and flowers, above
which floated the banner of their own country
entwined with that of Japan.

It was nearly 11 A. M. when our party arrived
outside the Town Hall, where a large crowd was
listening to an address from the Governor, con-
gratulating the Emperor and Empress on the
great work promulgated, after which the children
of the primary schools sung the National anthem
in front of the building. Fireworks were by this
time in full blast and were continued without
intermission for three days. The designs were
beautiful and wonderful, but their beauty could
not be realized until night wove her dark lines
about us. Many pieces were sent high in the
air by means of kites, and then exploded; others
fired from mortars would open hundreds of feet
above the crowd, and in sparkling light show the
form of men, women, flowers, and some even the
great Buddha on his lotus leaf seat.

During the day, the sky was dotted with kites
of beautiful shapes and designs, large and small
intermingled, some with bells giving a musical
sound, others with smaller kites attached in which
were placed pieces of glass to glimmer in the sun,
sending the rays about, and all keeping in regular
order. One feature was many large oblong
kites to which were attached a paper box for a
tail, filled with small birds, oftentimes canaries.
This, the manipulator of the string would con-
trive to fly just above the largest crowd, when by
a dexterous pull of the string, the box would fall
apart, the bewildered birds flying all about and
among the crowd. In the evening the kites were

lighted by beautiful lights and hundreds would
show the face of the royal pair as well as Yorotomo, Yoshitsune, and other rulers and founders
of Japan. Another feature of kite flying at
night, was to send up wheels, rockets, and other
fireworks, and when they had attained a suitable
elevation, by an adroit pull of the string they all
commenced to perform their parts until kite and
all landed on the ground.

The streets of the native town were everywhere crowded with shows and mountebanks,
and the windows of the finest stores and shops
decorated with their articles of trade, the finest
porcelain, the richest silk, the most elaborate
embroidery, and the beautiful carved ivory work
for which they are noted. The smaller shops
were decorated with ferns, evergreens and flowers, while even the trees along the street were
beautiful in their artificial blossoms of the cherry
and plum. At every door were two or more
flags of Japan, while at night, in addition, was
placed under each flag a lighted paper lantern on
whose sides, which were all white, was painted
the large red ball of the national banner, making
the streets resplendent with light and nation-
ality.

The Japanese traders, in anticipation of the
great event (probably patterning after their
Yankee friends), a day or two before the 11th
"cornered" the lantern market, not only buying
up the stock at the capital but at the places of
manufacture. The prices soon advanced, and
from twenty-five cents they rose to two dollars,
and the native papers reported that some sold
as high as five dollars before the festivities
closed.

The streets which had been full during the day
commenced to be crowded, until at three P. M.
the police found it impossible to keep the center

clear for the great procession which at that time started from the common, and began to thread its winding way along the principal thoroughfares of the city. In the advance came a small guard of some thirty men, dressed in the regalia of some of the ancient rulers, followed by a car, the center of which contained a tower which rose fifty feet in the air; it was decorated with oranges and other fruits, and flowers in contrast with the rich gilding of gold and silver of the car on which it rested. Seated on the top, in the Chair of State, sat Benten-the-beautiful, resplendent in her chair of gold, while stretching up the long column was the sacred dragon of Japan, with its head resting peacefully at her feet. Next in line was a representation of the Emperor and Empress, followed by the Cabinet, all dressed in the rich robes of State. In their rear were the deposed royalty of Japan, in the persons of the Tycoons, Shoguns, Daimios, and petty rulers. Then came the royal soldiers of each arm of service, the Army preceded by a native band, and the Navy by an improvised band representing the dress of many nations. Next to this came, on gilded cars, the trim man-of-war, the ungainly junk, and upon the deck of each were the sailors and fishermen of their respective craft.

Yokohama boatmen came in sampans, lustily using their oars, while a fleet of small fishing craft was dragged along, the occupants loading their boats with the paper fish which the boys hooked on their lines. Next followed large platforms on low wheels, with slight open work bamboo frames, in which were seated the singing-girls of Japan, each busy with the Samisen, Biwa or Koto, and occasionally above the music, which was exceedingly wild, could be heard the mournful sound of the voice, which even in its happiest mood is weird and solemn. In the rear of this came the same low cars and platforms without the bamboo frames, upon which were being enacted many an old legend of the country. The trappings were magnificent and the acting extravagant, but still beautiful and pleasing.

Where but in Japan could be seen theatres walking the streets, the actors unconcernedly playing their parts, the audience applauding, and the small boy shouting in the gladness of his heart? On one of the platforms was a tea-house in full play, the girls with painted lips and eyebrows shaved, hair elaborately dressed, and their silk wrappers and gorgeous *obis* (belts) tastefully arranged, all busily at work making and drawing tea, which with candies and fruits was passed to the crowd.

Then came a representation of all the trades in Japan. There were men from Satsuma plying their trade and polishing the beautiful ware of their province. Kaga and Hizen were not behind with their wares, which with the old and new porcelain of Imari filled the cars with beautiful effect. The Cloisenne ware was displayed from a car shaped like the heron or bird of longevity, and was one of the prettiest displays of the wonderful procession.

Other cars covered with food were, throughout the line, free for all to partake, but it seemed as if the abundance never grew less. In the rear were the coal diggers from Nogasaki, and the rice growers of the interior, with their scanty clothing and bungling implements of husbandry. From Hokadate came the hairy men, or bear worshipers of Yeso, leading their four-footed gods as quietly along the crowd as if they had been reared among a city populace. Then came on a car of state a monstrous white elephant, bearing upon its back a howdah in which were seated five girls, who were continually throwing flowers to the following crowd. The motions of this huge construction were sedate and solemn, and the swing of his trunk was in exact imitation of the living animal.

Lastly, came the fiery dragon of Japan, with wings aflame, and ready to swallow up all who straggled from the route, its motion being so much like life that it appeared to be a terror to the children who followed near its rear.

This line was over an hour in passing a given point, and at no time was a representation repeated, nor was there an exhibit that was not both beautiful and interesting. I have not mentioned half, as the reader will tire at my poor description of so gorgeous a scene. As night was now upon us we returned to our floating home, so as to be ready to start the next morning to see what new scenes would be presented to our eyes. At the end of the day we had all come to the conclusion that the Japanese did not need instruction from the enlightened West as to how to organize or marshal a procession.

CHAPTER VIII.

THE NO DANCE—KANAGAWA—STRAW WORK—
CEMETERY AND CREMATION—COURAGE TEST
—OKUMA SAN LETTER.

THE morning found us again in company with
our Japanese friends, speculating upon what
would be the order of the day, and wondering
if it could equal the celebration of yesterday.

We had not long to wait before the shouts of
the boys and girls were heard down the avenue,
as they rushed on ahead proclaiming the advent
of something new and pleasant. Soon there
swept into view a monstrous car, drawn by four
bullocks, on which was erected in evergreens a
huge *torii* or gateway, with many banners sus-
pended from it which bore the inscription in
Japanese characters, "Long live the Emperor,"
and above, on the cross piece of the *torii*, were
the words, "In Celebration of the Promulgation
of the Constitution."

Following came a bannered squadron with
flags and standards of all descriptions, rich in
silver, gold and gilt, with the words, "Long live
his Majesty, the Emperor." Then came the
shaven-headed priests of Japan, both the Shinto
and Buddhist being well represented, if numbers
are a criterion by which to judge, after which
was a long line of miniature temples representing
the different sects of each belief, as well as the
richest and most costly style of architecture with

which the temples of the East are adorned and beautified.

Many large idols on separate stages brought up the rear, and as certain noted ones would pass along the people by one impulse and seemingly one motion would prostrate themselves on the ground. Hundreds of children, from the little tot of five or six years, with head shaved in spots leaving the hair standing out like islands in a lake, to those of older growth, were banded together under the guidance of a priest with long sweeping robes and staff, who at every corner would join the mournful voices with the music of the weird bands in singing the national anthem, while swinging in the air a bouquet of the national flower, the chrysanthemum.

Flower stands of pine and plum blossoms combined with the camelia and rose, as well as baskets of flowers, some ten feet in height, brought up the rear of this grand line of beauty, and in a short time the street was deserted, the crowd following the line of march.

It seemed a pity that the procession could only be judged by its spectacular effect, as without doubt the extraordinary sights which passed in bewildering succession were emblematical as well as historical, and among which were woven many of the old legends of Japan.

We next drove to the common, where booths had been erected for theatres, wrestling-matches and other shows usual on great occasions; here we could also witness the celebrated No dance, the national dance of Japan, which has been handed down since the time of the Emperor Jimmu Tenno, 2,550 years ago, and is founded on an incident of his reign.

This Japanese dance is something more than a mere swaying of the limbs or movement of the feet. It is full of wild gestures and pantomime movements, which, without explanation from our friends, would have been deprived of the greater portion of their interest. They are really private theatricals without any dialogue. There are six dances, representing as many historical scenes, acted by gestures alone, the clue to the incident being furnished by the accompaniment, which had but little significance to us; but even without much knowledge of what we were witnessing the whole was highly interesting.

The costumes, which were of brocade and embroideries, were of the richest character that the olden days of Japan could furnish, and it was indeed a pleasure to witness what is not often visible more than once in the lifetime of an ordinary mortal. All was in keeping with the grand event, the music the best of the country, and the dancing the finest of its class.

I am indebted to the "Japanese Mail" for a description of this ancient ceremony, as well as the origin of the subjects of the dances. "His Majesty Jimmu, who was the leader of a band of invaders from the south, found his adventure opposed by numerous chieftains, among whom was the powerful and obstinate Yasotakeru. He entrenched his army in a well fortified stronghold in Yamato, and there defied the imperial forces with success, so that stratagem was at length resolved upon. The execution was intrusted to Michiomi-No Mikoto, a prince and leader. The inventive genius of the heroes of twenty centuries ago knew no quicker or surer means of luring a man to ruin than the charms of a deceitful woman. Such an one enticed Yosotakeru with his principal officers to a carouse in the tent of his enemy Michiomi, who, when the entertain- had reached its climax, stood up and sang a stave, the refrain serving as a signal to a picked band of imperialists who rushed in and slew all the visit-

ors.   A song of rejoicing concluded this sanguin-
ary scene.

Seven songs however were introduced into
the dance, which some centuries after Jimmu's
reign, when Japanese history was beginning to
emerge from the region of myth and allegory,
took the name of Kume-No-Mai.   Its observance
soon after fell to the house of the nobles Otomo
and Sahaku as an hereditary duty, and has been
kept in the line of their descendants until the
present time.   By these chosen members from generation to generation the tragedy is reproduced,
with all the peculiar paces, postures, precision
and spirit of a life-long occupation, and of late
years performed only at the coronation of each
succeeding Emperor.   The dances were eight in
number and the players on the koto two.

The representatives of the House of Otomo
played the koto, while the House of Sahaku performed the sword dance, with its included pantomime of slaying the rebel chieftains.   The
second dance was of Chinese origin, being a re-
production of the No or Sword dance, said to
have been performed by two celestial worthies
over eighteen hundred years ago.   The third
dance is called *Dakyu-raku,* and in this the dancers are dressed in equestrian costume and carry
staves, with which they go through the motions
of playing polo.   The last dance, called the
Kocho (Butterfly), was inaugurated in the year
906 A. D. and was composed by a Prince of that
time.   The dancers wore chaplets of flowers and
imitations of butterflies' wings, and look very
fine in their novel attire.

All was very interesting, and a better under-
standing of the circumstances upon which this
most clebrated ceremony of Japan was founded
and a knowledge of the details, made the scene
one never to be forgotten.

The third and closing day of the exhibition, although it did not fail to present novelties, lacked the zest and vim of the two preceding days. The bridges were adorned with as many flags and lanterns, the street, as well decorated and lighted, more dancing stages and theatres were at the street corners, but the processions were made up of the leavings of the past; the detestable jugglers and mountebanks, as well as beggars, were in every street, but the interested spectator had gone home, the exhibitor had lost his eloquence, and even the small boy, as night settled over the city, had departed, and so we likewise turned our steps homeward in a musing mood, our minds full of the past, wondering if it was all a dream.

A few miles across the bay lies the first designated seaport of this province, Kanagawa, which is worthy of a visit, and I asked my kind friends to accompany me there.

As it is the first station reached after leaving Yokohama, our steam horse soon landed us there, and we began to look about for the straw-work manufactory, the place being noted for its straw industry. We were soon informed by our guide that there was no one particular place, but that all the female portion of Kanagawa were experts, and employed themselves in making the many useful and ornamental articles which we had seen in the Yokohama straw stores. We gained admission to one dwelling where six persons were plaiting the straw for mats such as are used on the floors of all their houses. Some were braiding, others were weaving and sewing the pieces together, while some were filling the inside with a coarser straw and quilting the same, all busy and intent on their work, so much so that scarcely a look was given us.

Next we visited families working colored

straws of beautiful tints and finest texture from which they were forming toys for children, among which were beautiful plumaged birds which if you touched them ever so lightly gave forth a musical sound, while others with long beaks would whistle in imitation of the street boy; among the works were many beautiful boxes opening in unseen ways or not opening at all, unless the secret spring were shown you ; and in every house of the many we visited, some peculiar work was shown us which seemed to be done exclusively by the people of that dwelling, not even an imitation being attempted by the others.

The temples here are small and unpretentious, except one which is dedicated to education, or rather to the person who many years ago resolved the hieroglyphics of the Japanese into syllables and letters and founded a vocabulary, so that it became possible for foreigners to learn the language easily and translate the same readily. This shrine is much sought by the scholars of the surrounding country, and is well supported by the well wishers and liberal educators of Japan.

The receipts for the last three days, while the festivities had been in progress, were large, and at the time of our visit the priest and attendants were emptying the coin, mostly a small copper piece with a square hole in the center called "cash," into a sampan, which was at the time half loaded and certainly contained not less than three fourths of a ton.

This was to be sent to Tokio, where it was to be exchanged for coin of larger amount, and the small pieces (cash) would be exposed for sale at an exchange, where the people could buy this money for the gods, as it is not used in traffic among the people. The grounds along the temple front and river-side were tastefully laid out and several pretty trained trees added to the

beauty of the place. After seeing all that was
of interest we visited the cemetery and had explained to us some of the customs of this people.
This day many people, especially ladies, were
scattered over the grounds seeming to be enjoy-
ing the neatness of the plots, and the verdure
which had sprung up everywhere, even in the
tiniest little nook where the sun's rays could penetrate, and which here and there had blossomed
out a violet or dandelion, and they certainly
had all the appearance of a picnic party.

This surmise was quickly dispelled by our companion, who told us that it was the custom of all
Japanese to go to the cemetery on a certain day
of each month, to work among the graves of their
friends, adorn the surroundings, and on each
occasion wash the stones or head boards at the
tombs, so as to prevent the moss and dirt from
growing upon them. Even the rudest board or
rough stone where a mark was not seen to desig-
nate the deceased, was as clean as soap and water
could make them : all this turned my thoughts
to many a country place of burial in our own
country, where the homes of the dead never
receive such careful attention.

We next turned toward the crematory, which
was but a short distance away, and were in time
to witness a group about the building, who, we
were told, were mourners, and had come to see
the last rites performed over a friend who was
then in the furnace heat. They appeared to be a
jolly crowd, and acted more as if they were en-
joying a festival, than attending a funeral. Cremation has been practiced for some time in
Japan, and it is said that nearly forty per cent. of
the lower class of Buddhists, or monto sect, are
burned. The building was a rude affair, more as
I should imagine the sacred altars of the Egyp-
tians were, except that it was walled around, so

that when the body was in the heat it was not visible, but the stench which issued from the top was unendurable and caused us to hasten away.

Those who are not cremated are buried in a sitting position, the poorer class in tubs or a sort of barrel, usually what are called sake tubs. These tubs are about as large as a fifty gallon cask and two thirds as high, in which the liquor made from rice and called sake, is first sent to the market. After the liquor is disposed of they are in demand for coffins, as the liquor has served to preserve the barrel and is supposed to do the same for its inmate. The rich as well as those of rank are buried in the same position, but in a square box, sometimes several enclosed, one within the other, and their bodies are preserved from decay by filling the nose, ears, and mouth with red paint. If very wealthy, vermilion is used and the coffin is filled to the brim with the compound. On the day of burial incense is burned in the temple of which the deceased was a member, and he enters Paradise under a new or accompanying name, which is recorded by the priest.

As this is so dismal a subject I will close it by describing a pastime of the boys, who seem to be the same boys the world over. It is a test of courage, and called Kondameshi. A number of boys during the day plant several little flags in different parts of the graveyard, under a lonely tree or by a haunted valley or hillside. After dark they meet together and tell stories about ghosts, goblins, devils and other harrowing tales, until the imagination is highly wrought up, when the boys one at a time must go out in the dark and bring the flags, until all are brought in. Woe to the timid heart who fails to respond to the test.

As this is the last we shall see of our lady guide, I will add to the close of this chapter a letter received by my family from her shortly after our arrival in America, which may interest some one who will read these " notes."

The words enclosed in brackets are mine.

YOKOHAMA, August 30th, '89.

Misses C.

Miss Grace.

My Dear Mother.

My Dear Sister.

I remember you always of your kindness and your likeness with all my heart.

I expect you come next year, I am waiting for you. I suppose that mother will be come, but Grace-san (Miss) she cannot come, Oh! Oh! I am very sorry, very, very, sorry.

I would like you come Nipon next year with together Captain San (Mr.) Ohamisan (Madame) Grace-san, and Grace-san Goteishu (husband) if you can.

Grace-san : I remember always and I am living you all day and night ; every evening I will tell for your likeness, every time remember you with all my heart, please you guess my heart.

In Japan this summer very hot, so I was go Hakone (bath) between three weeks and I return yesterday evening (29th) therefore I cannot write of all my speak. My brother gone to Owari of his own business and he will return about five days from now.

My mother and brother give they best regards and many good wishes for their health and happiness to you Okamisan and Captain. I will write you next month.

I hope you have got all well home long ago and hope you will not get sick for a long time to come.

We speak plenty of the pleasant times we had with you and your parent. Dozo tegami us. (Please write.)

With much love and the best wishes for your future I am yours most lovingly

KUMA.

Please you come next year, I am waiting for you and I will send we likeness, please send me you family picture.

Dozo negai mas

K.

CHAPTER IX.

"GEORGE WASHINGTON"—FEAST OF DOLLS—
FEAST OF FLAGS—PRODUCTIONS OF JAPAN—
LACQUER WARE—PAPER MAKING.

As one wanders along "Honcho Dori," the
principal street of Yokohama, his attention is
called to a life sized portrait of George Washington, painted upon wood and placed over the door
of an unpretentious shop, which upon closer in-
spection will be found to bear the name of the
American General and Statesman, on the glass in
front.

All Americans are likely to stop and see who
the person is, and upon opening the door they
stand at once in the presence of the Japanese
who has adopted the cognomen of the "Father
of his Country." He is not at all diffident, and
will quickly tell you his name is Okabeda, that
he loves the American people and has placed the
name and familiar face of the one who was "first
in the hearts of his countrymen" where it can
easily be seen, and serve as a talisman to draw the
American traveler to his humble dwelling. He
is both genial and intelligent, always striving to
please, and at the same time glad to pick up
every English word that is spoken in his hearing,
and desirous to learn its meaning also. In this
way he has become quite proficient in speaking
the language. His small store, in which he is as-
sisted by his wife, is full of the many pretty
things seen in the shops of Japan.

His beautiful embroidery on screens and banners worked upon silks and satins, as well as other articles of needlework, are his pride, and they are as fine as any in the city. Many an hour have I watched him at his beautiful work, catching a word of Japanese in exchange for the English he was treasuring up, until we became quite friendly, and in time he and his wife were invited on board. As he had never visited a ship he readily accepted the invitation and set a time when he could come, which I afterwards imagined was a "red letter day" in his calendar. When the hour arrived I was notified that he and his family were on deck, and I hastened to meet them and gave them a hearty welcome.

They had already shed their shoes at the door, and as they entered the cabin each in turn dropped upon their knees, bowed their heads three times to the floor, repeating a Japanese formula, after which each handed us a present, it being the custom of the country to always make a present on the first visit. In Japan almost everything is counted by fives and tens, ten being the Japanese dozen, so we each received five articles of different make, then followed handshaking, after which a short time was spent in conversation, and then they were shown about the ship. If their pleased looks and bewildered manners were an indication of their enjoyment, their pleasure must have been great.

Before leaving, a cup of tea was served with sweets, of which they seemed pleased to partake, but not until they had slid from chairs to the carpet, did they seem at ease. On leaving, "George" said that in a few days, the third of the third month, there would be a yearly celebration or dolls' day, and promised to explain the doings and show us the entertainment, gotten up expressly for the girls and baby girls of Japan, if we would at that time visit him, which we gladly promised to do.

When the day arrived, we were made welcome by our Japanese friends and soon seated on mats in their parlor or best room, which for the day was under the supervision of the girls of the family (three) and their girl friends. On one side of the room, arranged on steps one above the other, were all the dolls and articles of dolls' attire, and the toys such as girls delight in, that had ever been given each little one since the year of her birth, and it would be considered a sad breach in etiquette in a friend not to send a gift doll to every little Miss under ten years of age on this festival day. Some of them were beautiful and the numbers were many, but as we seemed to be in the way of the little ones' enjoyment, we retired to the shop, and our friend George gave us in his best English a history of this " Feast of the Dolls," as the day is known.

Several days before the occasion the shops are gay with images which are on sale only at this time of the year. Every respectable family has a number of these, splendidly dressed, from four to twelve inches high, and which accumulate from generation to generation.

When a daughter is born in the house during the previous year a pair of images is purchased for the little one, which she plays with until she is grown up. When she is married, they go with her to the husband's house, and she gives them to her children, adding to her stock as her family increases. The images are made of wood or enamelled clay, but those presented by friends outside the family are many of them beautiful, as the era of fine dolls has even reached the distant East, and like many home people, each giver tries to do a little better than her neighbor. They are made to represent the Mikado and his wife, the old nobles of Kioto, and various personages in mythology and history. A great many other toys representing articles in use in Japanese houses, the dinner service, the kitchen utensils, traveling apparatus, and costly apparel are exhibited and played with on that day. The girls make offerings of sake (rice rum) and dried rice cakes, to the Emperor and Empress, and then spend the day in games and in mimicking the whole round of female life.

In the afternoon the room was full of invited guests, girls, and all were deeply engaged in games. One game much resembled the American game of Authors. It consisted of some one hundred cards on which were inscribed stanzas or poems so familiar or celebrated as to be known in every household. A stanza of Japanese poetry consists usually of two parts, an upper and lower clause. The reader has half the clause on her card and the player having the card on which the other half is written, calls out and makes a match. Then the next in the circle reads from her card, and so on until all are gathered in. Those getting the largest number of poems win the game. The one who loses the last card is the dunce, and wears throughout the next game a paper wisp in her hair and a chalk-marked face. Another pretty custom is to plant in the garden at the birth of every child, a tree, which on the child arriving at maturity and marrying, is cut down and the wood made into boxes to contain the jewelry and little keepsakes of the married couple.

To offset the enjoyment of the girls the fifth day of the fifth month is dedicated to the boys, and by them considered the greatest day of the year. It is called "The Feast of Flags." The shops, previous to the day of the feast are full of toys and tokens for the occasion. They consist

of effigies of heroes and warriors, soldiers on foot
and horse, the genii of strength and valor,
wrestlers and jugglers. The toys are in keeping,
consisting of the regalia and equipments of a
daimio's procession, all things used in war, arse-
nals, flags, streamers and banners, as well as the
usual arms employed in actual service. A complete set of these toys is bought for every son
born in the family. As the old Japanese families
are large, the display on this day is extensive
and brilliant. Out of doors is erected a bamboo
pole for each boy, from the top of which is hung
by a string a large paper fish. The paper is
hollow, so that the breeze easily fills out the body,
which flaps its tail and fins in a natural manner.
This fish, *nobori*, is intended to show that there
are sons in the family, and when painted a peculiar color, that one has been born during the year.

The fish represented, is able to swim swiftly
against the current and leap waterfalls, and is
typical of the young man mounting all difficulties
to success and prosperity. The boys form themselves into companies and processions in imitation
of the old rulers, every boy with a fish flag, and
often contest with rival processions until one or
the other party loses all its flags, when they retire
to their stronghold, home.

As the Japanese are a fun loving people, they
have numerous games, and days devoted to
them, which takes the place of our plays and
games in America, and are entered into with so
much zest, that they far outrival us in mirth and
joy.

On my arrival in America what was my surprise to receive a short letter from Japanese
George, enclosing Christmas cards for myself and
family, and as it will show what a determination
to master a foreign language can do in a few
months, I here give it to my readers.

Yokohama Japan. November 6th. 1889.
Mr. M. B. Cook
    Dear Sir
    Marry Christmas.
              Here I enclose in the cards which I
wish to present to you in the remembrance of
                    Your Very Truely
    I hope you are well since you left here and guass that you
are arrived at your country safely at present, and we are
well too.
    Please you visit to my house again when you come here,
I will wait for you Sir

                Yours faithfully
              George Washington
                Mrs. George
                  No 16 1st.
                Honchio Dori

Among the most noted productions of Japan, rice will claim the first place. This is cultivated in and upon every bit of low, swampy land, and is even raised on the sloping sides of some of the surrounding hills, where plenty of water can be had for irrigation.

From this is made an intoxicating liquor called sake, which is almost the only intoxicant used by the natives. Although the total consumption is considerable it is said to be used sparingly. It is very fiery, and quickly overcomes one who partakes of it. As a class, the Japanese are scarcely ever found the worse for its use, and drunkenness is considered an everlasting disgrace. A drunken woman, if ever seen, becomes an outcast at once.

Both Irish and sweet potatoes are extensively grown and are of an excellent quality. Tea is the great product of the country, and while large quantities are used among themselves, more than six million dollars' worth are shipped yearly, to the United States alone. The raw silk exported to our country exceeds that amount.

It is noted in our Minister's trade report for 1887, that the United States buys of Japan annually more than fifteen million dollars worth of goods, and returns in payment not one of our many staple products outside of kerosene oil, which trade amounts to less than three million dollars.

On many parts of the coast an edible sea plant is largely collected and conveyed into the interior, where it is an esteemed article of food, especially in those parts where salt is scarce. Large quantities are dried, then pressed into bales of about two hundred pounds in weight and shipped to China, where a ready market is always found.

Cotton has been cultivated since early times, and in 1882 the government presented to the United States National Museum an interesting collection of cotton grown in several coast districts, with notes on the same. In the province of Settsu, the largest crop is raised, but it is not of as fine quality as that grown in Kanto or Kanai, while the cost of cultivation is higher.

Fish are plenty off the coast, and most of the natives of the seaports are engaged in catching them, for which there is always a quick market. In fact, fish and rice, washed down by copious draughts of colorless tea, are the main food of two-thirds of the people of Japan.

Porcelain ware, gold and silver ware, toys, embroidered silk screens, curtains, fans, and the famous bronze and shippo ware are such noted articles of export that they will need no further mention here. The many coal mines supply their steamers and cars with coal, which is fast becoming an article of export, an occasional cargo being shipped even to San Francisco.

The country is well supplied with building stone. Many of the mountain ranges throughout the country are composed of granite, and excellent quarries exist near Tokio, to which city there is communication by water the whole way.

In the province of Sagami there is a soft sand-
stone which is being used in and about Yokohama, very pretty in color and supposed to be
durable.

In Japan there is a great variety of woods,
some of them very fine. Some thirty-four specimens are found in the island of Nipon. The
Kiake is most in use for temple building, as it is
very hard and durable, and takes a fine polish,
showing a beautiful grain. The mulberry tree is
much cultivated, as upon its thick leaves the silk
industry depends. There are several varieties of
this tree, which are generally planted in small
groves on open ground, well drained. Some are
in leaf early while others are later in the year,
nature having provided food for the silk worm
throughout the season.

Their lacquer work is exquisite, the most beautiful of which is made in Hakodate. The pro-
cesses through which it passes are both tedious
and numerous. The results are wonderful for
accuracy in every detail, many of the designs
representing plants and flowers, being worked
with so much care as to be in many cases botan-
ically correct. Particularly is this the case with
the raised gold work on wood. During the last
few years it has sadly depreciated in value, so
much cheap lacquer has been manufactured for
the European market. There are two varieties
of trees from which the wax is obtained, the
urushi or lacquer tree, and the urushi yama or
wild lacquer tree. From the first named the varnish or wax from which the lacquer is prepared,
is collected in bamboo pots, neatly formed from
the joints of the useful bamboo tree. At a certain season of the year the wax tree is cut hori-
zontally through the bark and the little pots
hung at the bottom of each slit, which as soon as
filled are replaced by others. In this way it is

collected rapidly, and needs but little preparation to fit it for use. The wax of the wild lacquer tree is obtained from the fruit with which the branches are heavy in autumn. The fruit is pounded up in a rude stone mortar and then shaken in open baskets, so as to separate the rind from the seed. From this rind the wax is made. The sifted rinds are then placed in hempen bags and steamed, then upon a table pierced with holes over which is passed a heavy wooden roller, the expressed varnish being collected in earthen pans placed under the form or table. The wax is purified by continual melting, after which a little oil is added, thus making it ready for use. The poorest quality is used as a fertilizer, the inferior quality for candles, which show a bright white light and burn slowly. The best is used for lacquer ware and also to wax the hair of the ladies.

The manufacture of paper was understood by the Japanese centuries before it was known in Europe, where people were forced to use for communication, leather, cloth, plates of lead, wooden and wax tablets, and even bricks and stones, as well as the bark and leaves of trees. They first used for that purpose the bark of the kaso, or paper tree, from which in time they produced a paper equal in strength to parchment.

This shrub was grown exclusively for its bark, which was peeled from the tree, soaked in water, then beaten to a pulp, after which it was well washed and cleansed. This being done, a portion of the pulp was taken up in small trays with low edges and spread over the dish by hand, the water escaping over the edge. Then it was dried in the sun and ready for use. This paper being made by hand, the sheets were necessarily small but smooth, and covered with a glaze derived from the bark, making a paper superior to that of any other nation in the early ages. Now they are as expert in their manufacture as any other nation, having extensive mills in which they use immense quantities of rice straw, making a tough, flinty paper. When combined with linen it makes the finest paper for books and writing material. The paper used for their bank bills is not excelled by the paper made for the same purpose in the United States.

In decorative art they are true artists, and their groups of well chosen, delicate flowers, their lifelike birds and their own gorgeously arrayed figures cannot fail to please the most exacting.

CHAPTER X.

EDUCATION—NEWSPAPERS — MUSIC — RELIGION
—DRESS—FANS—ODD CUSTOMS.

A PERSON hears so much and sees so many foolish and superstitious acts of the Japanese combined with their senseless idolatry, that he can but imagine them a very ignorant race, which certainly is not the case. The country is full of institutions of learning, and all places of importance have large libraries, which are well consulted.

One library at Osaka was visited during the month of July by 1900 people, by whom over four thousand, eight hundred books and volumes were inspected, many of which were in a foreign language.

As early as 1872 a law was proclaimed which provided for schools, one for every six hundred inhabitants, and in 1874 this law was in full operation except in the most out of the way parts of the Empire. At the present time English is taught in all the public schools of the cities, and there are at Tokio, Yokohama, Osaka, Kioto and Nagasaki as well as at other places in Japan, large well-conducted schools where many languages are taught, as well as the sciences. These schools are supported, as they have been built, by public generosity.

The girls and young ladies of the country are much indebted to the Empress for the interest she has taken in their education, and many of the schools have been encouraged as well as honored by her presence. Authors and poets are numerous, and are even honored in their own country. At a gathering of the same last year at Kioto, there were over one thousand present, while some three thousand poems, essays and compositions from those absent were submitted for examination and criticism.

There is one book of greater importance to the ladies than all others. The Hiaku Nin Isshin, a collection of one hundred poems by as many poets, written in an old dialect, and learned and repeated by old and young. It is on all subjects ; lives of model women, household lore, rules and examples, useful knowledge, ornamental instruction, music and love. This book is studied and committed to memory by all the daughters in every respectable family, until it becomes to them what the Bible is to many a family in our country, the first and last and oftentimes the only book.

In fact, Japan is the land of poetry, and it is a common thing to express the most trivial feeling of the day by a line from some native poet.

There are numerous papers published in Japan, almost as many as in the little towns in Maine, as the Japanese are as anxious to see themselves. in print as our enlightened home brother is. They have no less than eight papers devoted to medical interests, followed by nine devoted to sanitary affairs. Twenty-nine endeavor to popularize science, while thirty-eight are published in the interest of education alone. The news and sensational publications are numerous throughout the country. Some are not only printed in Japanese, but in English, German and Chinese as well. In 1889, an illustrated paper with colored illuminations, similar to the " Judge " and " Puck " of New York, made its appearance and was well received and supported. Surely if the publication of many books and papers is any indication of intelligence, these people are far advanced in wisdom.

One can hardly realize the vast stride this nation has made, when the mind turns back to 1858, at which time the first treaty was framed and this wonderful land opened for the first time to other nations, although even then foreigners were restricted to three or four ports. Now with but little trouble and no danger, the country can be traversed its whole length and breadth, and if you are so fortunate as to be an American you are treated with great respect and shown all courtesy, certainly more than many enlightened nations will deign to show.

The English language is spoken in almost every shop and store, and a person cannot get so far into the interior, but what the familiar words of his native land will reach his ear. At every seaport the click of the electric telegraph is heard, connecting each city throughout the Empire as well as sending its lightning flashes to Europe and America, for even in that far Eastern land some "Cyrus has laid the cable."

The railroads are forming a network in and about the island of Nipon, while the telephone is in use in every city. Gas lights their streets and dwellings, and the electric light is not unknown. While so much has been accomplished many things remain yet to be done, and the people have yet to learn the senselessness of their worship, the paying tribute as well as bowing down to wood and stone, before they can feel like one of a fraternity among the nations of the West.

The Japanese views and opinions in regard to vocal music differ widely from those of an American, and it would seem that this delightful pastime is regarded by the men as a part of a performance in which it is beneath their dignity to take part. It is very rare to hear songs from men except those of the very lowest class. The great majority of songs are sung by girls, and there are but few families in which the wife and daughters cannot sing and accompany their songs upon the koto or samisen. The men are not less fond of music than other nations and hence, no doubt, has arisen the custom of having at all the tea houses of pretension, professional singers to entertain the guests with vocal and instrumental music. The music usually commences with a low chant, weird and wild, which after a breath or two appears to have run down, then will suddenly start afresh like a cheap mechanical toy which has just been wound up, and the same operation is continually repeated, and in a short time you begin to doubt if any American ever admired Japanese music.

The religion of Japan is divided into two great parts or societies, which are denominated Buddhism and Shintoism. The first was evidently introduced from China, and is full of moral dogmas which are far from being cultivated by its believers. The Shinto religion is also claimed to have come from China or India by some, but as a general thing it is looked upon as a Japanese invention. The term "Shinto" is said to mean "The way of the Gods."

The disciples of Shintoism say that the Chinese were a very immoral people, and Buddhism was invented by them as a check upon their great immorality, but that the Japanese being a good people, there was no necessity for any system of morals, as everyone acted aright if he consulted his own heart. The original belief was a veneration of the common source of life, the fire light, or sun, which was considered the generating power. In time it was found more convenient to divide this power into many different parts or forms, and give to each a special *kami* (god) as its representative.

In ancient times the priests were always the chiefs of tribes, or heads of families, while their houses were the first temples. The Sun Goddess was always kept in the Mikado's palace until the time of Jimmu Tenno, when a temple was built to protect her worship from even his gaze.

Sacrifices were offered at first by killing animals and birds, but in later years they were carried to the altar and set free, and ever after were considered sacred. The Japanese bible, Kojiki, is said to contain no system of morals, no ethical questions, prescribes no ritual, nor points to any gods as objects of worship. This work is acknowledged by even Japanese historians to be the work of a female peasant. This woman was possessed of a remarkable memory and could repeat all the traditions she had ever heard, so, when in 712 A. D. the records were partially destroyed by fire, and ceased to be worthy of credence she reproduced the ancient religion from the beginning of all things to the present time. A noted writer, Mr. Mori, considers the leading idea of the Shinto system to be a reverential feeling towards the dead. He says, "little to-day is known of Shintoism which might give it the character of a religion, as understood by Western nations. Nothing can be found in it referring to the idea of a future life, while the fact that horses, cows and servants were buried with a deceased chieftain, go to prove a belief in a continuation of existence in another world after death.

Dr. Hepburn, after a thorough search among their most sacred books, could not find anything that could command respect, and concluded it was more a department of the Mikado's government, and a means of working upon the minds of this superstitious people, than anything else. At the present time it is being swallowed up in Buddhism, or, at least, the two faiths are becoming confounded with each other, while both are being shaken to their foundations by the stride the nation is taking in spreading her educational system, which is fast rooting out the old impure rites and ushering in the new, or rather the true religion of the more enlightened nations.

As at every place one enters, if he intends to conform to the Japanese custom, he must remove his shoes, a description of the same may not be out of place. The slipper, or common sandal, used only by the poorer class, consists of a sole made of rice straw, slips of rattan or of wood, without upper leather either at the front, or the heel. The front is crossed by a strap covered with cloth and fastened in the center of the sole near the toe. The strap passes through the great and second toe, keeping the shoe fast to the foot. For this purpose the stockings are made with a thumb like a mitten, giving a separate place for this important member. When it rains, or the roads are very muddy, the shoes are soon wet through or worn out, so that along all the principal roads worn out shoes are continually seen. Many, in the rainy season, wear a high wooden clog, hollowed out under the middle, with band and toe string as with the others, thus they can walk without soiling their feet, which are usually covered with a low white linen sock called *tabbi*.

The shoes of the better class are strapped in the same way, but many are strangely carved and elaborate in lacquer. They never enter their houses with shoes on (and it would be an act of extreme impoliteness for a stranger to do so), but leave them at the door, so that they are always in their socks or barefooted in the house and no dirt is carried in to the neat mats with which all their floors are covered. The mats are so common that it has become a current expression in Japan that they build their houses and divide them into rooms to suit the size of the mats of the market.

Their dwellings have no stationary walls except sometimes on the outside, but the rooms are divided from each other by carefully made light screens or sliding doors running in grooves, to which they are fitted. The slight frame work of these doors is covered with a thin, tough paper, generally oiled and oftentimes painted in fanciful designs or even lacquered, and is the chief thing inside of many of their substantial dwelling houses. The oiled paper also serves to admit light, glass not being in common use except among the wealthy.

The rooms contain but little furniture, generally a chest of drawers to hold their bedding during the day, a shrine, which is in every house, containing one or more hideous idols over which they chin-chin (pray) often, and always when about to retire or rise from slumber, and an oblong box, about three by one and a half feet in dimensions, partly filled with sand, upon which they build or always have a charcoal fire, over and around which they hover, joining each other in a social smoke.

It is hard to tell which they relish the best, tea or tobacco, for one or the other, the tea cup or the pipe is constantly at their lips when a company of them are gathered together. Even in making a call on a neighbor the ladies never forget to take their pipe and tobacco.

If I could describe the ladies' apparel it would no doubt be of interest to some, but not being versed in ladies' attire I shall have but few words to say. In a criticism on an English book re-

garding Japan where an allusion was made to
their barbaric dress, the *Japan Mail* replied thus:
" The Japanese, whose highly civilized lives were
regulated by the strictest codes of refined etiquette, dressed in silken raiment and practised
the fine arts in an age when the writer's ancestors
lived on acorns and covered their nakedness with
untanned hides."

Their outer garment comprises a whole dress
called *kimono*, which covers from the throat to
the feet. It has very large flowing sleeves, so
long as to cover the hands, the sleeves being
used as pockets in which to carry their handker-
chief, fan, or small parcels. The upper part
which forms the sleeves crosses over the back
like a small cape, which serves for warmth as well
as for comeliness. About their waist they take
several turns with a long silk band, nearly a foot
in width, tied in a large smooth knot behind, the
ends tucked in out of sight, thus forming at the
same time a wide belt and large bustle. It is
upon this article of dress that they are most inclined to outdo their neighbors. This one orna-
ment supplies to them as regards finery what a
spring, summer, or winter bonnet does to an
American lady. It is made of the finest material
and elaborately embroidered, and even the poorest of the people would look with indignation on
a waistband of cheaper material than fine silk.

Even their *kimonos* are always silk or linen,
even if the wearer goes barefooted and lives on
rice alone for months to obtain the coveted dress.
As they never wear a covering for their head,
their hair is dressed and waxed into many fantas-
tical and often beautiful shapes, then filled with
valuable gems in the shape of pins, with brilliant
carved heads, representing beautiful flowers and
other creations of nature.

Their stockings of white linen only cover the

ankle, and one of Clara Belle's letters states that
if a pious missionary who spent ten years of his
life among this people and learned all about
them, can be relied on, the Jap women wear no
underclothes whatever under this single outer
garment. The people being small, their style of
dress is always becoming, and they look far more
graceful in their own attire than in the European
attire which they are beginning to adopt.

It has been said that " fans were not invented,
but grew in the shape of broad leaves." If one
can let his imagination extend back to all ages
there might have been seen even in the Garden
of Eden our first parents, sitting under the tree
of knowledge, slowly moving the first great leaves
to circulate the air and cool the hot winds of that
vicinity. As time advanced and improvements
increased, they became ornamental and of rich
material as well as fanciful in design, and now at
this late day it is claimed by the Japanese that
they were not only the first inventors, but the
first to introduce them into polite society. At
present, in their country, they certainly occupy a
very important place in the attire of a lady and
are in use by most of the gentlemen of the land.
They are of all kinds, from the light bamboo,
split and covered with cheap paper embellished
with fancy and comic pictures, to those of very
elaborate make, framed in beautiful wood, ivory,
lacquer work, and even in silver and gold, then
covered with the finest and most costly silks,
satins and so forth, and all elegantly embroidered. They are seen in the hands of all classes
of society and are cherished as a sacred thing by
men, women and children. At their public exhi-
bitions they are given as prizes, also at school as
presents, as well as on their new year's day and
state festivals. You are ushered into their homes
by a wave of the fan, called to lunch or waved

away when your visit has expired, and instead of raising the hat in the street on passing a friend, the fan is used as a token of recognition. Often your money, when making a purchase, is received on a fan, and the change, if any, returned on the same. In fact, it is the one thing which the Japanese are at a loss to be without, and also the one thing of their attire which is always gracefully used and seems to be a necessity of their dress.

At the marriage ceremony it was formerly the custom to gild the teeth of the bride with some corrosive liquid, after which they always remained black, and serve to show that a woman is either married or is a widow. This form in late years has in a great measure been dispensed with, so that now the distinction is not so readily made. The people can marry as often as they please, and any relation except brother or sister. I have read in some home paper and had the facts confirmed by an old resident of Yokohama, that when a family has a marriageable daughter to dispose of they allow her to suspend a flower pot in the window or on the veranda, in which the Japanese lover, as soon as it is seen, hastens to plant some choice flower, which is equivalent to a proposal to the young lady. If he is the one she cares for his gift is carefully tended by herself, that all may see that the donor is an accepted suitor. If he is not, the plant is torn from the vase and will be seen soon after withered on the path below.

The most important article of dress for a Japanese bride at her wedding is a long flowing piece of gauze, white and soft in texture. This is prepared with great care and is woven by the bride and her intimates. It is used only twice, first for the wedding veil, and again when at her funeral it serves as a winding sheet.

" Weave ye the veil, O maidens ! soft and slow
  Your strains may echo here ;
Twine strong the thread and firm the weft let go,
  To last for many a year ;
The bridal robe, with all its graceful flow
  Must drape the funeral bier."

CHAPTER XI.

HIOGO—HORSE TEMPLE—WATERFALL—OTSU—
MIIDERA TEMPLE—LEGENDS OF THE BELL
OF MIIDERA—NEWSBOYS—INARI TEMPLE—
POETRY AND PROVERBS.

IT was my good fortune while at Yokohama to
find a friend wishing for company down the coast,
on a proposed visit to Kobe or Hiogo, and the
surrounding country. His cordial invitation was
gladly accepted, and we were soon on our way to
see more of Japan and its many wonders. Nothing of interest transpired on the way, unless the
beautiful scenery up the Kii channel, and the
numerous fishermen in small boats in Hiogo Bay,
which nearly blocked the way, might be mentioned as such.

The foreign settlement at Kobe is finely laid
out, with wide, clean streets, but was of too modern construction to cause any exceeding surprise.
Hiogo, the old town proper, was done in jinrikisha in a day, and was only an old town with
thousands of thatch-roofed huts spread over a
large, low flat, and outside of its numerous temples and a few theatres, was dull as well as disap-
pointing to the eye. The principal temple was
enclosed by a high, stone wall, the only entrance
being a huge gateway open to the East. The
court of the same was large and spacious, some
forty rods in length, at the end of which was the
edifice for a mammoth red image, which appeared
to be the attraction for all native visitors. This

was covered with paper balls or chewed up prayers, which the people buy at the gate, chew to pulp as they walk up the court, and then throw at this august body in red lacquer, and if the symbol is fortunate enough to stick, the prayer sender goes away satisfied. By the pile of pellets lying around the base, we concluded many must have been disappointed, and had retired to buy, chew and throw anew.

Both sides of the space leading to the temple are lined with booths and stalls, tea houses, archery galleries and mountebank shows, and in the evening when the lights are shedding sparkles of brilliancy on everything, the scene is truly delightful.

To the north of the town is another old temple of dilapidated appearance in which is kept an old white horse, and by Americans this place has become the Horse Temple. It is an old structure, and has for many generations had for its chief deity a white horse. On the death of the animal an exact counterpart is made in wood, whitewashed and placed in the temple at the head of the enclosure, where they are fed daily, often with cakes, rice and sweets, food more suitable for the priests than the quadrupeds. After the death of one, the country is scoured until another is found bearing certain marks, when it is hailed as a promise of Buddha, and is brought to this temple with much ceremony. About the yard are women and children selling beans, oats and corn to visitors, who, on buying, are allowed to feed the sacred animal. After every mouthful has been swallowed, the horse gives you a solemn nod, and some say winks his eye to the priest in attendance, indicating how well he has taken in the giver.

Above all, and a few miles out of Kobe, on the highest elevation of the surrounding mountains, is the Temple of the "Moon." It is unpretentious in size or adornment, but is held in much reverence by the people, on account of some old and sacred legend connecting it with the past of the country. From it a beautiful view of the bay and country is had, while far away across the bay the towers and steeples of the temples of Osaka can be seen.

The waterfall, one of the attractions of the place, is very fine; whenever there is a rain shower, it dashes down many a steep descent, and of the three falls which it takes while worming its silver thread down miles of rocky gorges, one is really magnificent. The head of this wonder of nature is a small lake in the far mountain's top, which overflows enough in the driest season to show a glimmer of silver light as it races down to the sea. I was warned by an old Japanese not to follow up the waterfall to its source, as he said it was inhabited by a sacred dragon which it was death for any one to look upon. On my return he shook my hand heartily, and said he was afraid he would see me no more, and then related a number of cases where visitors had gone confidently up the summit, and were never beheld by mortals again. Upon close questioning he owned that of late years there had been no tragedy connected with the ascent. But for all that, all the wealth of Kobe would not induce him to make the trip.

In the older part of Kobe is one long, narrow street filled with the beautiful wares and curios of the country. Among the most beautiful was some straw work made across the mountains, and found for sale in profusion in Kobe. The straw was used for mosaic work and for covering small ornamental articles, in which these people are experts. The work is executed in so perfect a manner, that it excels in designs and workmanship that of all other countries. Small boxes for jewelry, made of native wood, then veneered with colored straw, forming various patterns, are very common. Some of the articles are exquisite specimens, and very brilliant in color.

Having satisfied our curiosity about Kobe, Hiago and the near vicinity, one morning, just as the first light in the East spread its golden rays on mountain top and glistened on the gilded god of the Moon temple, we found ourselves on the cars rattling over the country towards the little town of Otsu (Oats), situated on the shore of Lake Biwa (Beaver), which we reached early in the day. Here we took jinrikishas for the noted temple of Miidera. Leaving our teams at the base, we toiled up over four hundred steps, and on reaching the summit, could gaze in admiration and wonder at the little city of Otsu at our feet, and the beautiful lake before us, reaching farther than the eye could pierce, while away to the left was the high mountain of Hira, with its snowy crown, resembling Fusi Yama in its cold grandeur, upon which the sparkling sunlight shone gloriously, causing the lake to reflect its miniature waves a thousand times in its bright, refulgent glow.

The temple itself was a beautiful specimen of art, with turrets, mounds and monuments covering many acres of ground, the whole forming a scene one could not appreciate alone, but needed friends to gaze with him and admire the wonderful view and the new beauties which meet the eye at every turn.

Up this high, rough mountain, with steps in many places cut into the solid rock, had been brought a bell, famous for its weight, antiquity and story. It had its wonderful legend, as all things in Japan have. In old times the casting of a bell was a great event, and performed with

much ceremony. It was a common thing for
ladies of quality to present the mirrors (steel,
glass being unknown), which reflected their
charms, to be melted down and become incorpo-
rated with the bell, in expectation that every
time it was tolled, it offered up in sweetest tones
a little prayer that the donors be forgiven their
follies and frailties. What prettier idea was ever
cherished? The sweet chimes of the bell at even
wafted on the wings of the wind to the gods, be-
speaking favor for the fair ones below.

The bell was also considered a very holy object. To pass under it was a deadly insult to the
spirit of the bell, and a man was turned to water,
while a woman became a devil for the offence.
This "great bell of Miidera," as it is designated,
is remarkable in many ways. It is some twelve
inches thick, and about twenty feet high from
top to bottom, while it is only six feet in diameter across the mouth, and resembles an old-
fashioned, bell-crowned hat, minus the rim.

One of the legends is that in olden times this
bell was thrown into Lake Biwa by some demon
opposed to the temple authorities, or the Deity,
who was supposed to preside over it, and that for
twelve hundred years it could not be found, when
an earthquake raised it nearly to the surface,
where a fisherman discovered it. For a number
of years every effort was made to raise it from
the lake and convey it to the shore, but without
success. When the Japanese were in despair
about getting it to their temple, a heavy fall of
snow filled the lake, chilling and causing the
water to congeal except about the bell, and the
next night, amid peals of laughter and mirth, a
giant strode down from Hira (the god of snow),
lifted the bell from its watery bed, carried it up
the high hill, and placed it in front of Miidera
temple.

A spot is pointed out where there is a little hollow in the metal, caused, it is said, by the celebrated beauty who, struck with admiration of its polish and beauty, laid her hand upon the bell and prayed aloud for just such a mirror to reflect her dimples. The bell, as if outraged by the speech, withdrew from her touch and left a hollow, where before there was roundness. Could it have been that the melting pot received no contribution from her and the guardian spirit was angry in consequence?

Whatever its faults, inconstancy was not one, for another legend relates that Benkei, a giant, renowned for prodigious strength, stole the bell from Miidera and carried it to his own place. Then it changed its chimes to the most profound melancholy and longed so for its old home that it had but one burden to its song. Let it be rung ever so often it would only sob out from early morn till dewy eve, "*Miidera ye iko*," "I want to go back to Miidera," until Benkei, provoked by its repeated complaint, shouldered the bell and carried it back from whence he took it, flung it down in disgust, since which time it has become a reasonable bell, and its chimes have become more musical than before.

A little chapel has been erected in which the bell is hung stationary, and is now rung by a small timber, in a box or groove made for the purpose. When a number of persons force the timber rapidly against it, it gives out a deep, sonorous tone, like some far distant harmony of nature. A few pennies will secure the privilege of pushing the beam, and every sound the casting emits are so many prayers wafted somewhere for your welfare.

The lake, dotted with islands, was covered with boats of all descriptions. Moving about on its surface were many side wheeled steamers, while no less than ten were made fast at the docks. After gazing delighted at the superb scenery we reluctantly turned toward the town, where we soon arrived, under the skilful guidance of our Japanese muleteers, and then took a boat and shoved out into the lake to try our luck among the fishes with which it abounds. Success crowned our efforts, so that in a short time we were again on the shore, our fish in the hands of a Japanese cook who, in half an hour from the time we embarked, had the results of our sport before us nicely boiled, and that alone, except the inevitable cup of Japan tea.

Here we found the first newsboys we had seen in Japan, and they cried the "Otsu Journal" as lustily as the boys of New York ever sung "'Ere's your papers" on election eve. Of course, all foreigners buy, and although not a word could be read, or a word that the boys said understood, we nevertheless bought all the papers they had. To see their roguish faces as they scampered away with the few cents they had earned, and no doubt remarking on the simpleness of Americans, was pleasure enough to have caused us to invest much more in the, to us, unreadable pages. While here we were warned away from the tea house (the first and only time) on account of an illustrious Jap who was leisurely sipping his tea, and we were told that it would be no less than sacrilege to intrude while he was so employed.

A few bits of porcelain were added to our collection as a remembrance of the place, and then we took the train back to Kobe, stopping at Inari, and having the pleasure to look over the temple of the same name. The Inari temple is the head temple of a certain sect of the Shinto religion, and the only one of note in this section. It is a magnificent structure and at that time was crowded with devotees.

Inari—or the "benevolent God Inari," as he is more commonly called, is the "God of Rice," and no husbandman would think of planting his rice, upon whose yield his life almost depends, without courting the smiles of this beneficent god by an offering of food, in some instances, and in others a paper prayer bought of Inari's representative, who stands at the temple gate with large piles of the printed slips to sell to every devotee who wishes to secure the good will of the benevolent.

Here I was fortunate enough to find a little pamphlet printed in English, containing a few short stanzas of poetry and a number of old sayings, or Japanese proverbs, in fact, a real old Richard's Almanac without the calendar. As they may interest some reader I have added a few of them to the chapter.

" I have been familiar with the flowers
  Yet are they withered and scattered ;
  The beauty of the convolvulus, how bright it is ;
  Yet in one short morning it closes its petals and fades.

" When the roaring waterfall is shivered by the nightstorm,
  The moonlight is reflected in each scattering drop."

  " Wonderful are the frogs!   Though they go on all-fours in an attitude of humility, their eyes are always turned ambitiously upwards."

  " Since Buddha thus winds himself round our hearts, let the man who dares to disregard him fear for his life."

With one of the most common I will close the book of poetry.

  " The potter moulds the clay upon the wheel, and behold, a jar, valued at a few cents.
  The artist takes his brush and decorates the jar, and lo, the piece is worth the ransom of a great warrior."

Of the many old saws or maxims in the little book, most of them appear familiar, although differently expressed, as the following :

" With time and patience the leaf of the mulberry tree becomes satin."

" It takes a thousand years for muddy water to become clear ; so with a soiled reputation."

" A great measure is carried with great contention."

" To hear one side is darkness."

" When there are two spirits in the sky a rainbow is produced."

" You cannot quench fire with charcoal."

" The hen that crows in the morning brings misfortune."

" The truth of what is within appears upon the surface."

" The good or ill of this world depends upon the heart."

Many more might be transcribed, but with the following I will close the old saws and the chapter.

" Heaven has a voice which is heard upon earth, for the walls have ears and stones tell tales."

CHAPTER XII.

IT was with much pleasure that myself and family received pressing invitations to join a party of excursionists on a visit to the city of Kioto ; so one bright afternoon in March we started from Hiogo, a jolly party of eight, including our Japanese guide, Yoshi, whom an American friend had kindly procured for us.

The day was fine and fair, our party in good spirits as well as agreeable, and we were fortunate enough to get a division of the car to ourselves, so at once commenced to enjoy the landscape, scenery and passing wonders, noting the many different styles of dress and customs of the people at the way stations at which the train stopped, and, in our exuberance, we began to think we owned the cars, if not the most of the road, when, to our surprise and disgust, a Chinaman forced himself among us. His pipe, which he attempted to smoke, was probably picked up near Osaka, but we had to endure his company until the next station was reached, after which his chair was vacant.

We were next greeted by the voice of an American, for whom we gladly made room, and found him both amusing and entertaining. As he had lived in Japan twelve years his knowledge of the country was considerable, and he appeared to be glad to impart a portion to us, but not

until, Yankee like, he had found out all the par-
ticulars about each, even to the date of our birth.

Before we arrived at Kioto he left us, and we
were sorry to part with so genial a traveler. A
little after dark we entered the ancient city and
took jinrikishas for the noted hotel Yaami, situated on the side of the mountain Maruyama,
which lies directly east of the city, of which it
commands a beautiful view.

The long, even streets, lined with huge square
blocks of buildings, show a great constrast to
the average Japanese towns. Cherry and peach
trees, full of blossoms, perfumed the air; while
many shrubs and flowers just bursting into bloom
imparted their delicious odor. The sides of the
mountain are dotted with numerous tea-houses,
gaudily painted and decorated, the gardens
around them beautiful in walks, arbors, artificial
lakes and flowers.

This being a favorite resort of many of the
city inhabitants, it is a profitable business to the
proprietors, as their visitors can sup their tea leisurely, while listening to music and watching the
graceful motions of the dancing girls, who are
one of the attractions of the place.

The hotel is large, roomy and nicely kept, the
walls about it grand, and the attention paid to
guests would be an innovation in many a hotel in
our own land.

A warm fire, a nice bed and refreshing sleep,
followed in the morning by a delicious breakfast,
and we were ready for the pleasures of the day.

If the reader will first let me transcribe a few
lines from an old book relating to this place, he
may take more interest in following us about as
he reads this imperfect sketch.

" Kioto, for centuries, has been and still is considered The Sacred City of Japan, and from 793,

A. D. until the departure of the Mikado for Tokio, some twenty years ago, was recognized as
the supreme capital. The political capital under
the dynasty of the Tycoon, was wherever that
ruler chose to reside. It was supposed when in
its most flourishing condition to have contained
nearly two millions of inhabitants, but, at the
present time, even including many small villages
on its borders, to have less than one million people living in about two hundred thousand houses.

The floating population was very great. Many
of the Daimois, or feudal lords, were obliged
to repair to the capital at certain periods to pay
their respects to the Mikado, some of them
traveling with not less than three thousand re-
tainers, and such cavalcades were not of rare
occurrence."

At this date, when all the influence of royalty
has departed, the city still retains her ancient
grandeur and keeps her bright place in the es-
timation of the nation by the magnificence of her
temples and the display of her notable monuments, but mostly by the sacred character which
is attributed to the former residence of the Supreme Ruler.

There are estimated to be one hundred temples
controlled by three hundred priests of the Shinto
belief—the religion of old Japan—while there are
about two hundred and fifty temples, supporting
over twelve thousand priests, who are the followers of Buddha.

Seven thousand dancing girls live in different
portions of the city, and no party, feast or excursion is complete unless some of them are employed for the amusement of the guests.

Kioto is also known as the place where the
four gods live, from an expression made by a
noted ruler who ascended the mountain to over-

look the valley and choose a place on which to erect imposing buildings and a noted castle for the Imperial residence.

When he saw that portion of the plain called Udamura and its surroundings, he was so struck with its beauty that he exclaimed in ecstacy, "Ah! this is truly a place where the gods dwell;"—for, according to Japanese legends, there are four great constellations: in the East the dragon, in the West the tiger, in the South the bird, and in the North the serpent and the tortoise. Hence the exclamation; for he saw the river Yodogawa running through the city represented the dragon, while the mountains by which it is surrounded he likened to the other three heavenly bodies.

Here the buildings were erected, and the walls of the Imperial palace, which were destroyed by fire in 1653 were made so extensive as to include the dwelling houses of many of the people, and it was said by old chroniclers that the palace alone occupied over two hundred acres of ground. Since that time the Mikados have been contented to live in castles of smaller dimensions.

When the capital was first removed from Nara to Kioto, which was done by Tenno in 793, he caused the image of two renowned warriors to be buried at the foot of some tall trees near the base of one of the mountains, and it was believed that if the city was invaded by an enemy, the two warriors would shake the hill to alarm the people, and rise from their tombs to help the people repel the invaders.

This mountain is a prominent landmark, as it has three clumps of trees on its summit, which have been trimmed to resemble a ship under sail. From an elevation near the hotel, the river Kamagawa can be traced from the gap in the northern hills, and its silent, silver stream followed the whole length of the city. This river is crossed by many bridges, some of them noticeable for their architecture and massive blocks of stone. One called Sanjo is of interest to the traveller, as all distances in and about the city are reckoned from its center. Excepting a twinkling thread of shimmering water, the rocky bed was nearly dry, the clean white stones along its shores were covered with cloth, bleaching for the different factories which are situated on its banks.

Away to the southwest the temples of Honganji, with their flaring roofs, make a decided feature on the landscape. But to return to our party, we find that our guide has already engaged jinrikishas for us, and we were soon winding our way across the valley in our little carriages, each drawn by two Japanese in tandem style and all strung out in single file, making a long line as we go at a fast trot across the ancient city. We are soon in the suburbs, every eye gazing at the beauties of nature, as seen in mountain, lake and ravine, which in this delightful weather seemed to have taken on new beauties, or else our hearts were so light with present and anticipated pleasure that all the world seemed joyous and beautiful.

We passed many people with their loads of wood, bark, hay, vegetables, and various other articles of traffic, all heading for the city, the most of them seemingly overloaded with their heavy burdens. All, or nearly all, were hauled by the people to whom they belonged, being loaded upon a long bodied cart set upon two wheels so as to balance, the cargo being placed in the same manner. At every little hill they doubled up their human teams as is often done at home with oxen, then a hard pull, accompanied by the words *Ye Sai Chiyodzura,* repeated over and over, until before the day was over they became a by-word to the clown of our party. After our return we found it to be the rallying cry of the celebrated priest Ye Sai, who was the founder of the noted Zen sect as early as 1202.

Since that time laborers lighten their burdens by repeating his name, coupled with that of one of his followers.

Soon we began to climb the long ascent between the mountains, gradually getting higher and higher, for be it known we are bound for the unimportant town of Kameyama, at the head of the Rapids of Oigawa, down which we expect to shoot with all a traveller's enthusiasm and the cataract's velocity. The ascent at last gets too steep for our Japanese teams, so we unload ourselves gladly and run ahead up the ever rising grade. On the way we buy oranges (ten for a cent) to throw at the children we pass, and who often disdain to pick them up, for they are plenty in every hut. Sweetmeats are another thing, and the little, wee bodies with their black, bead-like eyes will follow a long distance for a drop of sato (sugar) which some of us who had a little were glad to give them.

We soon reached the top, took our seats in our little chaise, and were whirled through the dilapidated village, turned an angle at the end of its only street, which brought us at once to the head of the navigable part of the rapids, the waters of which were rushing after each other down a fall of many feet. Here shoal boats some thirty feet long and six wide were engaged for the downward voyage, into which we all embarked with our jinrikishas and drivers, who were right glad to rest after their pull of fifteen miles in less than three hours, and the most of that over rising ground.

Here, as elsewhere, the maid of Japan was ready to serve us with tea before we pushed off, so after

a cup, and a word of farewell, away we dashed
into the seething and whirling waters.   Soon we
were moving along the first stage, a plane of
comparatively smooth water, probably one half
mile distant, when we entered a narrow gorge
where the river becomes rocky and the current
very rapid.

> " The cataract strong
>   Then plunges along,
>   Striking and raging
>   As if a war waging
>   Its caverns and rocks among."

Two men then took their places at the bows,
one with a short oar, which he hung in a rope
rowlock on the starboard side; the other had
armed himself with a long bamboo to push us
away from the rocks.   At the stern were two
other boatmen who controlled a long sweep with
which they could turn the boat quickly, good
management being all required, as the current was
swift enough at all places to carry us along without other propelling power.

At first, we could hardly divest ourselves of
some slight fears as we saw the boat rushing at
an alarming rate to what appeared certain destruction on the rugged rocks, which seemed to
encircle us on every side, but with a push of the
bamboo in the bow, in concert with a sweep of
the long oar at the stern, we swept past all dangers, escaping some seemingly by a miracle.   If
we had not been informed by our guide that an
accident never had occurred, our fears would have
been much increased.

We have never witnessed anything more magnificent in its way, than this wild river gorge.
The high banks on each side are beautifully
wooded, and as the river twists and turns in all
directions, we seemed to be entirely surrounded

by sharp, rugged rocks and verdant hills, the brown and green of which were sprinkled with the bloom of the first flowers of spring, while a roaring cataract was whirling and dashing under us.

As we glided along, our boatman sang snatches of Japanese songs, always ending in a low, sweet whistle. Soon, away in the far distance up the mountains, from the glens and down the stream would come a musical answer, when in a short time from every rock and bush could be heard the sweet song of birds in exact imitation of our sailors, each one trying to rival its mate, until the air seemed alive with music sweet as an angel choir. For a few moments our men would remain quiet, then again send a low trill out into the surroundings, when in an instant the feathered warblers would be all about us, filling the air with their delicious notes. Neither did they leave us until we were at the end of our race, which was successfully accomplished in less than three hours, the distance being about thirteen miles. Our boat often grazed the rocks, but suffered no danger, as it seemed to have the rebounding propensity of a rubber ball. After a delightful passage in which every moment was enjoyed, we rushed down our last and most dangerous declivity and emerged into a basin at the foot of the beautiful mountain Arashiyama.

This high mountain towering above the stream, which has here lost its grandeur and flows placidly at its base, is famous for its luxuriant growth of cherry and maple trees, the blossoms of the one and the red leaves of the other attracting crowds of visitors during the summer and autumn.

We disembarked on the left bank of the rapids, almost in the garden of a tea-house, up the stairs of which we were ushered, after we had complied with their request, politely given, to take off our shoes, before we were allowed to put our foot on their smooth lacquered floor. Then our lunch, which we had brought with us from Kioto, was spread before us with the addition of the delicious oranges of the country and the inevitable cup of colorless tea.

The whole trip was extremely exciting as well as fascinating. The wild scenery, combined with the pleasurable feeling one enjoys while passing down this mountain gorge would be hard to describe. One of our party, who had served in the cavalry arm of service during the rebellion, said it came the nearest to a grand successful cavalry charge of anything in his past experience.

Here some of the male members of our group were much amused when they saw one of the tea-house girls dancing about arrayed in the wraps of our lady companions, and were no less so on departing to witness the frantic efforts of one of our Japs endeavoring to button a lady's boot with a hairpin. He must have wondered at what no doubt he called our high civilization. If he did not we knew by his expression that he was won dering why he undertook the job.

CHAPTER XIII.

OUR human teams having fed and watered, we again started them on our journey, this time in the direction of the city, by the way of the famous temple of Nishi (west) Honganji, at which place we arrived early in the afternoon. Seeing so many temples as one does who visits Japan, he soon becomes so accustomed to them, that they are not noticed except where they are especially elaborate in workmanship and design, or noted by having some history or old legend connected with their existence.

Such was the case with Honganji, which was founded by a descendant of the first Mikado in 1260, and is said to be the largest and finest in all Japan. It is placed in the center of an elegant garden of forty acres and surrounded by a neat, handsome wall. In this enclosure the great Japan exhibition of 1872 was held, that did so much to bring the great trades of the Empire to a common center and develop such unknown wealth.

There are many beautiful buildings scattered around the grounds as there are in all the temple grounds, no one building comprising the temple but "all are parts of one stupendous whole," making a resort for pleasure as well as worship. On the south side of this enclosure is a very elaborately carved gate, designed by one of Japan's most noted artists of ancient times. It is considered particularly sacred and is only opened to admit the Mikado.

In the Hondo (main temple) is a beautifully executed statue of Shonin, founder of the Monto sect, to which this temple belongs, carved by himself, while in the other buildings are many idols carved by the most skillful workmen. In a side room are several life sized pictures in oil of the principal priests of this sect, as well as other propagators of the Buddhist faith. These temples are built of the finest and costliest materials, while the most skilled mechanics were employed in their construction. The shrines and pillars appear to be one mass of gold, and the carvings, by celebrated artists of their time, masterpieces. In front of the Hondo is the famous icho tree, noted throughout Japan, very large and very old, and which is believed to vomit water from every branch during fires in and near the temple. As they have never been visited by the scourge, they ascribe their immunity from the same to the protection this tree affords.

The priests of this sect are the knights of the order, being allowed to wear swords, and not restricted by rules regarding their diet, and in former times were permitted to marry.

At one side of the main temple is the pleasure house of a Japanese noble, enclosed in the temple grounds and again by a separate wall, inside of which is a fine garden and one of the seven sacred springs of water for which Kioto is celebrated. In the garden is a stone called Yakosekki, said to be luminous at night and to draw its fire from the icho tree near the temple front. In one room of this building are life-size pictures of some forty famous poets, dating from 1210 A. D.

But to return to the main temple, where we were ushered in by a shaven crowned priest, who very kindly took us in charge, giving us much information through our guide regarding the priesthood and this edifice. At this time the several departments were controlled by fifty regular priests, under whom were three hundred students, preparing for their life vocation.

First we visited the room sacred to geese, in which were pictured on ceiling and panels geese of all sizes and painted in all positions, and so natural that one could easily imagine that he was in the midst of a flock, waiting expectantly to hear them hiss, then on to the next room adjoining, which had for its patron saint the stately peacock, and these were, like the geese in the room we had left, painted in gorgeous colors, but natural as life. We then passed through a narrow hall to the land of flowers, represented by paintings on wall and ceiling of the large room into which we were ushered. The first room, as the most important, was devoted to representations of the chrysanthemum, which is the national emblem and is interwoven with the monogram of the Mikado. The scene was beautiful, and one in which a painter of flowers would delight to linger. Next we passed along a gallery by the side of the building, across boards of keyaki wood, over five feet in width, so contrived as to make a whistling sound, and at every step they uttered a weird moaning, until we came to the tiger room, covered with ancient paintings of this royal beast as well as some carved in wood, all very life-like and interesting.

We then followed our ghostly guide in his long sweeping robes along another hall and across wide boards said to be laid upon large earthen pots, which gave forth a sweet sound and are called "the singing boards," to the head priest's room, which is alarmed from without by the music made by the visitors' feet as they cross this temple organ. In this room is a wonderful picture of the moon shining through a soft haze on the grand pinnacle of Fusi Yama, the sacred mountain. Here also was exhibited the dais on which the Mikado sat when he visited the temple ; its exquisite carvings and fine paintings, almost concealed by gold is beyond effort of mind to describe.

Among the noteworthy objects explained to us were the thick mats by which the floor of this room was covered. These were made in sections of some four by nine feet in size by eight inches thick, the outside woven from very fine rice straw. The inside was filled with alternate layers of raw silk, each thread crossing the layer under it until it was the required thickness. This was to protect the priests or any one claiming their protection, as in times past under the old régime many were obliged to do.

One noted priest who sought this sanctuary was killed by his enemy, who got under the building and ran his sword up through the floor, so these mats were stuffed with silk and made so thick that no sharp instrument could pierce them.

But our jinrikisha men are tired of waiting, so we leave the beautiful rooms, delightful gardens, and enchanted ground, and travel to the east to visit the sister temple Higoshi (East) Honganji, which was partially destroyed by fire a few years ago. It is now being rebuilt by the citizens of the city. It is of massive proportions, the new part elegant in carvings and designs. It is expected it will take four years to finish it ready for use.

This branch of Buddhists is reputed to be very wealthy, and comprises among its members those most able to support their cause and furnish funds for the same. The building fund is collected by the priests, and we were informed that if necessary, they could collect a hundred thousand dollars in the course of the day for that object. The work, which seemed to be well advanced, was supported by many huge pillars of a native wood called keyaki, some of them four feet in diameter, beautifully polished in their natural color. About the top were carvings emblematical of the tenets of their faith. We were shown two ropes, each 360 feet in length, one three and a half and the other six inches in diameter, the larger weighing over a ton, both of which were made of human hair. It was indeed a curiosity, not only because of the manner in which it was made, first in small braids, then rope laid, after which the small ropes were cable laid, making it as firm and nearly as hard as iron, but the dark hair of the maiden was mixed with the gray locks of age, while the short locks of the young men could be traced beside the long, straggling locks of the old, making the whole length one continual mixture of the old and new, gray and black, soft and shining, and coarse and lusterless.

All this had been a voluntary offering, and not only the members of this temple but the whole city felt it an honor to contribute to the erection of this grand building.

This hair rope was used in erecting the gigantic pillars and placing the massive beams, it being believed that with this material for a purchase no accident could happen.

The people of the temple have full faith in their creed and are doing much to advance their belief. They have established schools in their temple grounds in which they mingle with their own language that of the English, and are at the present time educating forty young men who give promise of talent as missionaries, to send to America and Europe to propagate their faith. They have also built a temple and school near Shanghai, China, and are there educating forty priests with a similar object.

I fear my readers may find too much about temples in my writings, but as everything in Japan, whether in history, legend, or romance, has priest and temple connected with it, they must bear with me for a short time while I take them over this historic city, but first to the re-nowned temple of Sanjusangendo, which was built in 1162 in honor of Senjo Kwanon (one thousand hand god) and contains one thousand idols of large size. Each idol is surrounded by a number of smaller ones, making the total number 33,333. The largest is a sitting statue of Kwanon, which is eight feet from the knees to the head, and carved by a famous carver named Kokei. The one thousand idols are arranged in tiers on each side of the larger figure and repre-sent gods and goddesses, each having its particu-lar fable or legend, the whole completing a nar-rative of touching incidents. On one side of the temple was a dilapidated shooting gallery with a range of two hundred and forty feet, and not-withstanding the great distance for archery pur-poses, it is a matter of record kept by the priests that some wonderful matches were held here. The temple in times long past, must certainly have been a fine building, but now nothing but the gods are kept in proper repair.

The main building faces the east and has a length from north to south of three hundred and ninety-six feet. There are thirty-three mas-sive columns running the length of it through the center, of grand proportions, carved at foot and top, and resplendent in lacquer of a reddish

tint, making a sharp contrast with the idols,
which are covered with gold leaf.

In front of the Hondo is a sheet of water said
to be covered with a small purple flower every
year in the month of May, making the place attractive.

In connection with this temple, tradition nar-
rates that the builder suffered from an excruciat-
ing headache which caused him to make a long
pilgrimage and pray to many gods ; at last, while
performing his devotions, a god appeared to him
saying " go back to Kioto and consult a skillful
doctor who has just arrived there; follow his
advice and the headache will cease. He did so
and prostrated himself in prayer, when the doctor
appeared to him as a god, and told him he had,
in a former life, been a noted priest and traveler,
and in his next would become Tenshi, one of the
sacred gods. He also told him that when he first
died his bones were put into a box and thrown
into the river, where, in the course of time, everything but the skull decayed. That still remained
at the bottom of the river Iwata in Kishiu. The
trunk of a willow which grows from the river
passes through the skull, and when the wind
blows the tree moves to and fro causing pain to
the head, and that if he removed the tree his
headache would cease.

The suggestion was followed out with the well
prayed for result. Out of gratitude, he built this
temple and placed in it the skull as an object of
worship. The willow tree, which was one hundred and ninety feet long, he used as the top
beam of the edifice.

We next visited a place called Dai Butsu, where
we arrived late in the afternoon, too tired to admire, but after a short time returned to our hotel,
and I will record what information was received
from our guide while spending the evening there.

This building was erected by a noble of the time of Tenno in 1587, and the largest idol in Japan was built and placed in it for the people to worship. It was a Buddhist figure called Rushanabutsu, constructed of wood, and measured one hundred and sixty feet from base to head. The edifice in which it was placed was two hundred feet high, one hundred and sixty-two feet wide by two hundred and seventy feet in length. This image was broken and the building partially destroyed during an earthquake which took place a few years after its erection, killing many people and flooding the eminence on which it stood, by the outrush of water from the many openings made by its force.

The donor and builder was angry with the image which he had built to protect the city and which was not able to protect itself, so he shot an arrow into it, then totally destroyed the remains, and at great trouble and expense brought an image from Shinano and put it in its place. This not bringing the prosperity he expected to his native city he replaced it in 1603 by a bronze idol sixty-three feet in height. Shortly after the temple was destroyed by fire, and again rebuilt by the son of the founder in 1611, and at the same time a large bronze bell was cast for the temple front. The image, which was defaced by the fire was taken down in 1848 and melted into *cash* (a copper coin, ten for a cent) many of which are yet in circulation distinguished by the figure (X, *bun*), a contraction of the day and year in which they were made. Two years later another wooden idol took its place, which was destroyed by lightning, and not until about fifty years ago was the colossal statue which now adorns it, put into its present home. It has been affected so unfavorably that people in a great measure shun the place, and the few priests are not able to

keep it in repair, so that it is but a wreck of former days. The bell is twenty-four feet high and
ten inches thick, and has had almost as variable a
fortune as the temple and its gods. On the
South side of the bell is the following inscription:

"The steep roof of my temple is high up in
the blue sky and its crystalline base reaches to
the bottom of the earth. Its thousand pillars
and posts stand high with beams and rafters
placed upon them. Some parts are adorned
splendidly, and some parts are carved beautifully.
The stones about the temple are of great use,
and the little bells hang down from the eaves and
ring as the wind blows. The beautiful gate
stands loftily in my front and even the Deity
within bows down struck with its magnificence.
Besides all this I was made to indicate the morning and the evening hour. I open the ears of
mankind and the musical sound of my tolling can
be heard up to heaven and reaches down to hell.
The new bell hangs high. Its sound dwells long.
It reaches everywhere. Its tune is suited to the
general sounds. The ring of a thousand and eight
times grows slack. The rings of an hundred and
eight times are hurried. To light the lamp at
evening and to burn incense at morning even
India hears. The pure moon is welcome in the
East. The oblique sun is setting in the West.
At Ho the mountain frosts comes down. Tell
the matter to Kan, that the country may be at
peace. The virtue of the superior master is
higher than the mountains and greater than the
water ; and joyfully I ring—may the Mikado live
a thousand years."

According to the rules of the Buddhists, the
strokes on their bells always end with eight, and
as it was now the hour when the deep tones of the
bells all over the city came wafting up the hill, we

thanked our guide for the imparted information, gladly bade him good night, and retired to dream of the bells, gods and goddesses of the " Flowery Land."

And now that all are asleep I will append an incident which happened when in Kioto a year ago, and which, although not relating in the least to our travels, will be appreciated by many a lover of America, and in a manner illustrates the character of a certain class of all nations who are wandering through this empire, where they have acquired the significant name of Globe Trotters.

While spending an evening in Kioto with another Yankee captain, we strayed to the billiard room and engaged in play at the one table which the hotel afforded. Soon after, four English tourists came in, two of whom were gentlemen, while the other two were inclined to be snobbish. The two latter looked upon the game for awhile with disgust, wishing to have the table themselves, and evidently by their remarks and actions were looking for some way to mildly insult us. At last one of them backed up to the fire which was in an open grate, lifted his coat tails, with a deal of satisfaction, and remarked so loudly that we could not fail to hear —" This is the only thing an Englishman ever turns his back upon—a good fire in a grate."

The intent of the remark was so plain that it could not help being noticed, as it was, at once, by my friend, who turned to the Englishman and in a quiet manner remarked, " You must have forgotten Bunker Hill and New Orleans." It occurred to him as soon as he had spoken that there might be an objection to Bunker Hill, but there was no need to make a correction, for the fellow, muttering something, left the room, followed by his friend. His other two countrymen seemed to enjoy the retort, made our acquaintance, and we four passed a pleasant evening together.

CHAPTER XIV.

COMPLETELY refreshed, we awoke the next
morning just as the light of the east began to
spread over the valley city, and after paying our
respects to the miniature shrine of the Fox god
in the hotel yard, we ate a hearty breakfast,
called in our span and again started on a round
of pleasure.

We pass down the steep declivity and out by
the tomb of the ears and noses of the many prisoners captured and killed by an army of 150,000
Japanese when they invaded Corea, a few years
before the erection of this monolith in 1590.
The monument is 720 feet in circumference, and
about thirty feet high, named Mimizuka. Our
mind sickens at the tragedy and so we leave the
place and drive along a wide street to the entrance of the temple Otani, to examine the imposing entrance gate, Karamon, brilliant in fine red
lacquer, and in architecture superb, where we
crossed the spectacle bridge, so named because
of its resemblance to a pair of spectacles.
This neat piece of stone masonry crosses a
pond filled with the broad leafed lotus plants
and surrounded by cherry trees, beautiful
in their bloom, making many a quiet nook

and lane in which the traveller delights to linger.

We next hastened up the long street of Kiyo-midzu to a temple of the same name, and as we passed along this famous street, crowded with porcelain ware of all descriptions, we could easily imagine we were in fairy land. For nearly a mile, every door, street corner, stand, shop and store was piled full of the choice articles of Japan's beautiful ware. The finest and most fragile was exhibited, and all so beautiful that one could but gaze in admiration at the rich display. Some articles were so thin and clear that common print could be read through them, and although seemingly too fragile to touch were handled by the shop-keepers as carelessly as if it were heavier ware. Even in this city as well as throughout Japan, the plates, cups and saucers and tea pots made in this district are considered rare specimens of the potter's art and are the most celebrated of all in the " Land of the rising sun." It is not to be wondered that we broke one of the command-ments coveting the quaint and grand pieces we saw all about us.

At last we are at the temple gate and enter a place alike glorious and venerable to the natives, and a place which multitudes visit both for wor-ship and pleasure. The grounds are magnificent, although not so extensive as many others, while the temple is very old, having been built in 798, shortly after the establishment of the capital at Kioto. The approach to this sacred edifice is up a long flight of stone steps leading to the door. At its base is a tiny waterfall, clear and pure, which comes winding down the cliffs, stealing in and out among the shrubbery, until lost in its wanderings far below. A large stage or platform has recently been added to the structure, over-looking a depth of some fifty feet.

In front of the Hondo are several pictures, representing excellency in archery and horsemanship, while many offerings, prayers and petitions are hung about. At one side is a small shrine dedicated to the patron saint of true lovers. In front of this is a small grating to which strips of paper prayers are attached by unmarried people of both sexes, who desire the favor of some sweetheart. To make the petition a success the pieces must be tied on with the thumb and little finger of one hand. It was amusing to watch the bashful maiden of tender years attempting in a diffident manner to attach the strips, the blushes chasing each other across her face, while the older person or widow with much nonchalence and ease, as if it might be an every day occurrence, performed the deed.

A curious superstition connected with the place is, that any one jumping down from the platform without being killed will have his wish gratified. In former times many persons made the jump, most of them being killed. The last case took place some twenty-six years ago, when a young married woman, whose husband had proved faithless, threw herself over, followed by her maid servant. Neither was permanently injured but well shaken. The husband was so struck by her devotion, that he reformed and became an example to others for his virtue. This caused such a rush of wives to try their fate that the authorities had to put a stop to the experiments by building an impassable barricade of bamboo about the platform.

We next passed the beautiful tower of Yasaka, which being 120 feet high, rises grandly about the buildings surrounding it. This is of different architecture from any other in the city, being built in the style of Eastern pagodas, five roofs rising one above the other. The upper part was richly decorated, and the top, which was said to be plated with gold, shone like a yellow ball of fire in the sunlight. Being conspicuous as well as ancient, it is one of the first objects to attract a stranger's eye. The illustrious Prince Shiotoker erected it as an offering to Buddha, but religious prejudice led a mob to tear it down. After a time, the renowned Yorotomo caused it to be rebuilt and it now stands as the last work of the last of the line of the house of that great Prince.

Near the tower is a temple of the same name, at the entrance to which were hundreds of stone images, from three inches to three feet high, perfect in every detail, many of them highly polished and not a few dressed in fantastic clothing resembling dolls. Each had its alloted niche, the whole forming an interesting group and well worth a passing examination. One of our party tried to buy one as a memento of the place, but the bald-headed priest indignantly refused to sell. A few cents given him appeased his wrath and caused him to light two candles, which he set before the most sacred shrine as a peace offering to the gods, and for a small addition he rang the bell which stood before the altar, wafting a prayer for my wife and self to the Lotus Leafed Paradise. His looks appealed to the rest of the company for the privilege of doing the same for them if the few cents were forthcoming as an incentive. The Bismarck of our company refusing to contribute, we repaired to the inner room, where the gifts of the day were being gathered together, after which they were shoveled out of the sacred box into leathern bags to convey elsewhere. The day's collection had been large, there being more than a bushel of copper coins, among which were mingled a few pieces of silver. We were allowed to exchange some pieces for the sacred cash by making a small addition to their treasury.

After lunch and a rest we drove to the Imperial grounds called Gosho, the old residence of the Emperors. An exhibition of the industries of Kioto were being displayed at the time. The grounds, though much smaller than in former times, are still large and interesting, made so by the way the temples, buildings, trees, shrubs, and ponds are scattered about and arranged. In the middle of the open space, surrounded by an inner wall, still stands the building which was the seat of government and into which none were admitted except the high court officials. This enclosure, containing about five acres, is entered through one of the three massive gates, while the large space outside, enclosed by still another, or outer wall, is entered by any of six splendidly carved and ornamented gateways. The approach to each is magnificent, as the gates are resplendent in gilt, gold and lacquer, while much of the material of which they are composed is ancient bronze castings.

The school buildings were fine, the royal race course grand in its proportions, and the sacred stone monkey in a niche in the wall especially noticeable; this is supposed, by its superior cunning, to circumvent evil influences and keep them from entering the gate.

Our next move was to a Shinto temple, Kitano Tenjin, built in honor of a great promoter of the old Japanese religion and celebrated for his loyalty to his sovereign. The approach to the large temple building is paved with immense flagstones, and along the sides are erected a number of small tea houses in Chinese style, with prettily cultivated gardens in their center. Passing through these we emerged into a wide space or park of great size, then on between many tall bronze and stone lanterns, where at every few feet on either side were the images of horses, bulls, cows, or calves, some standing, others reposing, and all perfect in their sculpturing. These idols were life size and made of different material. One, a wooden horse, was so perfectly carved that the veins, sinews and joints seemed to belong to a live body instead of wood.

We thought of the siege of Troy, but doubted if the wooden horse of the ancients was as perfect as this one worshiped by the Japanese. Some of the imitations were in bronze, some of marble, and others of granite. One of a cow, made from a block of black stone, with here and there a stripe of dull red and yellow running through it, was a marvel of beauty and art. We gazed in admiration at these symbols of religious faith, so perfect in every detail, and wished much to know what creed these images represented and what could be the motive of the people in upholding so absurd a religious rite.

At the temple front we found nothing of interest except the priests stringing the pieces of cash which they had received during the day on to a crotched stick, as our eastern fishermen do their alewives when they prepare them for smoking, and a very large, polished, steel mirror, elevated at an angle in front of the main entrance. Many people were in front of this reflector, bowing and placing themselves in such a position as to cast their image in the mirror, after which, bowing their head three times to the ground, they went away feeling blessed, for they had had their own faces shown them, and as nothing repulsive was seen in the reflected image, they felt that they were all right and might now commit almost any sin, since Kitano Tenjin (Eye of Faith) had not destroyed their beauty.

As time was fleeting, we once more occupied

our little carriages and were hauled to Kinkakuji,
a temple at the foot of some low hills on the opposite side of the city. This is a large enclosure
of many acres laid out as a garden, where great
attention has been paid to the cultivation of various trees, flowers and plants, some very rare,
which grow here in luxuriance. The temple
stands in the center, almost surrounded by a picturesque lake in which are several little islands,
each tastefully arranged in different designs, as
the Japs so well know how to do, one taking the
form of a bird, another a fish, still another formed
like a temple with trees about it, yet another was
made to resemble in outline a vessel under sail,
the trees forming three masts, while the limbs
and foliage bent and trimmed the sails.

This building, erected over five hundred years
ago, is still in a good state of preservation, and
bids fair to outlast many generations. It is three
stories high, with a piazza around each story.
The ceilings and walls of the upper story were
covered with gold leaf, but the hand of time as
well as that of visitors have contributed to its
destruction, so that now but little of the leaf remains except under the eaves, where it is inac-
cessible to either destroyer.

A small fee was demanded at the gate for
tickets of admission, and a guide followed sharply
at our heels, fearing to trust us alone, so often
had their shrine been desecrated by western
visitors.

The lake is full of fish, and it is a pleasure to
feed them from the lower story with crumbs of
food obtained from the attendant priest. The
finny tribe can be called together by clapping the
hands, which starts them, coming from all directions, a mixture of many kinds, among them
many small turtles. As they cluster about the
temple steps they form a happy family, and,

although eating voraciously what was given them, did not attempt to devour one another. The veranda from which they are fed was the place where the founder cleaned his teeth, and made the inhabitants of the waters acquainted with his features. North of the temple is a sacred spring of sweet water, from which he made his tea, and near by a fall of water trickling down among the cliffs, where his ablutions were performed.

Just above the waterfall, on a small island in a pond, is a monumental stone covering the grave of a famous white serpent, which in ancient time made its home in the lake. Everything has quaint legends and stories connected with it.

Near the entrance is a pine tree, trained so as to perfectly represent a Japanese junk under sail, and showing a wonderful art in the fashioning. The Hondo, at the entrance of the grounds, is of large size, neat and tasteful in architecture, and contains many relics of olden times, such as ancient armor, priests' dresses, porcelain and swords of former rulers. On our return from the lake we were invited by the priests to partake of tea with them, and were regaled with sweetmeats and priest cakes, some of which we were glad to bring away as a remembrance of one of the most interesting places we had visited in the city.

Our visit ended, once more our biped steeds struck out at a swinging pace for the manufactory of the famous Shippo, or Cloisonne ware, where we soon arrived. We were ushered into a fine drawing room, where the first object which riveted our gaze, after the familiar cup of tea, were the many medallions, medals and certificates of the excellency of the work done here. Among them one issued at Philadelphia in the Centennial year seemed to bring us nearer home, while that as well as others reminded us that at every international exhibition since 1876, this far away Japan had competed successfully with all enlightened nations, every time securing the highest prize.

Some fifty people were at work, and it was an hour of extreme pleasure which we spent in examining the manner in which the gold, silver and bronze is put upon the copper, of which the foundation of the beautiful vases, plaques and other ornamental ware was composed.

Some of the work is of the most minute character, strong lenses being used in applying the gold and silver when forming the elegant designs. One could not wonder at the extremely high cost of this beautiful work, when the many days of labor necessary to furnish each piece are considered. A plaque, eight inches in diameter, was marked fifty dollars ; and a set of three small pieces not over three inches high, sixty dollars. Scarcely anything, except napkin rings, could be had for less than thirty dollars. A pair of vases was being finished for the Mikado, which, in beauty, were beyond anything ever witnessed except the works of nature.

Our next move was to the great porcelain works of Kinkozan, where we were kindly received and conducted through all the different parts, from the preparing the "clay well mixed with marl and sand" through the moulding rooms and to the "furnace flame," where the first baking takes place, then to the designing rooms, where numbers were intent on making those odd, fanciful figures and scrolls about which so many of our home friends go wild in their profusion of praise ; then to the rooms where scores were tracing those designs on elegant shaped urns, vases and other ware ; then through the long line of painters, who were delicately touching the figures with the long, flexible brushes dipped in paint which it would be a fortune to know how to compound ; again, to the furnaces where the firing takes place, and, lastly, to the finisher, who corrects all defects, burnishes them, and adds the last gold luster, when they are replaced for the third time in the fire, which finally ends the work and leaves in your hands a work of beauty.

How truly has our own Longfellow said:

> " The leaves that rustle, the reeds that make
> A whisper by each stream and lake,
> The saffron dawn, the sunset red,
> Are painted on these lovely jars."

It is useless to form a determination not to purchase for the temptation is irresistible, and each one of us was followed by packages as we left the manufactory.

The important silk weaving manufactory of Nishijin next commanded our attention. From the squalid appearance of the vicinity no one would imagine such beautiful fabrics as were displayed could be found here, but, as in many other cases, we found appearances deceitful, for we had the enjoyment of seeing them weave the figures of flowers among which gay butterflies and birds were floating in the heavy brocade silk, the natural colors of each delineated by the various shades of the silk threads employed, which were here and there intermingled with threads of silver and gold.

The gayest and most valuable dress goods made in Japan are loomed here. In the sample rooms, magnificent embroidery is exhibited as well as much fine work, both made by hand and woven. The beautiful waistbands and neckcloths, which all well dressed ladies wear, were here in profusion, being wonderful in figure as well as in fineness of texture, while some of them were stiff with silver and gold threads woven in, and others by the same material in embroidery. The goods manufactured here command an exorbitant price, as the name Nishijin is a guarantee of their being made from the best and costliest materials.

One more temple and our sightseeing for the day is done. This is Chionin, where we invest in maps of the ground and pictures of the large bell of which it boasts. Like many another, this is of ancient date, having been built in 1202, but has been destroyed and rebuilt so many times, that but little of the original temple remains. It is situated on the side of Maruyama, one of the highest mountains which encircles this lovely valley. The main building is a grand structure in the center of a large square on the highest parts of the ground, which affords a splendid view of the city. From the veranda which surrounds the building, the city is spread before you, with charming lakes, rivers and gardens intermingling throughout the valley, while the encircling mountains are enveloped in a robe of spotless snow, which has fallen during the day, causing the hills to look like radiant orbs of light, and as if already purified for the coming of the Lord. The lower part of the gardens are threaded by three long avenues leading up to as many gateways, along which are built a number of small houses, each . occupied by the priests of this order (Jodo) and each having a tiny garden in front of his house, also a place set apart in each yard (a cunning little house, set apart for worship and study.

Under the eaves of the Hondo is an old umbrella which was said to have been left there when the temple was finished, not being noticed until the scaffolding was removed. It has become an object of great interest to the worshipers and is almost as sacred to them as some of their gods. In front stands a large bell, sounded as is usual), by a beam running in a groove, but only rung on festival occasions or when visitors pay a few cents to the priests for permission to ring it.

By the side of the main avenue leading to the temple is a large stone which was said to grow lemons, which it produced in a single night. On each side was written the name of one of the host of the gods of Buddha.

This particular god was to be the chief object of worship until another was grown. At the gateway visitors will notice many stones lodged on the top of the same. There is a belief among the Japanese that if they throw a stone to the top and it remains there, their wish will be granted, as also the sticking of spitballs of paper on the huge wooden image at one side of the entrance will gain an answer to their requests.

After visiting so many temples, all of which have a certain resemblance, I cannot explain why Chionin showed more beauty than many others, but it appeared not to have been built but to have sprung suddenly up among the gray cliffs and tall trees, while the beautiful carpet of green about the grounds seemed enchanting, and the many little children playing in one part of the enclosure made the whole seem more what we have often pictured Paradise to be than any place or temple we had visited.

We climbed to the summit just above us and cast our admiring gaze over this vast edifice and the mountain bound city of Kioto, which the setting sun was making glorious with its soft, quiet light, and as we gazed, the thoughts would fill the mind that this was the East, the far Orient, and that it was beyond the power of man to picture from our western home a scene more fair. But the day is ended, so we hasten to the station, take the train for Hiogo and enjoy the evening ride as we chat about the many beautiful and grand scenes we have witnessed and enjoyed, as we have never enjoyed anything before.

In bringing my fragmentary notes to a close, I must say that to my mind the picture of Japan is a bright one. Up to the present time the people have shown great aptitude in adapting themselves to a higher civilization, and in very many things they compare favorably with the nations of the West. What their rapid advancement may lead to will be known in the near future. A people so amiable and clever can have only the best wishes of all who hail the advance of Christianity with a love that is second to none other.

> "It is ended!
> The last page has been written;
> And with reluctant hand,
> And with a lingering look,
> I close the well loved work.
> It is ended!"